Images in Colour

Images in Colour

Leatrice Eiseman

LITTLE HILLS PRESS

Dedication

To Herb, my dear husband, for his help and encouragement; and to Bea and Ben and to Lori for her beautiful photographs. To Ken and Aunt Lilyan, and the rest of my family and friends for being so supportive and such good listeners.

To Al, Muriel and John Hackl for loving colour as much I do. To Robert Hickey, my wonderfully creative Art Director, and his able associate, Chris Jones. To Kathleen Hughes, whose intelligence, grace and homemade pea soup have nurtured me. To Laurie Tag and Sandy Trupp for their good humour, friendship and hard work; my editors Valerie and Phyllis Avedon, and all of the other special people at Acropolis who made this book happen. To Dene Hofheinz-Anton, Shirley Webb, Christine Torres, and Stan Taylor for their special efforts; and to my fellow members of the Color Marketing Group for their assistance. To Kay Sarazin, Jeff Angell, Frank Westmore, and Vicki Sanchez for sharing their expertise. And to all of the marvellous clients and celebrities who gave me the gift of their time.

© Acropolis Books Ltd., 1983
  Alive with Colour

© This edition
  Little Hills Press, 1985

® Registration Pending

All rights reserved.
Except for the inclusion of brief quotation in a review, no
part of this book may be reproduced or utilized in any form
or by any means, electronic or mechanical, including photocopying,
recording or by any information storage and retrieval system,
without permission in writing from the publisher.

ISBN 0 949773 13 1

Contents

The Colourtime Quiz: Are You Sunrise, Sunlight, or Sunset? 7
Quiz Explanation 11

Part I *What Colour Can Do for You*

1 Discover the Secrets of the Colour Clock 17
The Sunrise Palette ... The Sunset Palette ... The Sunlight Palette ... Creating Your 'Ambiance' ... Exploding Old Myths ... White Doesn't Go with Everything!

2 Making the Colour Clock Tick for You 38
What To Do if Your Chair (or Hair) Is Fading ... Accessorising with Colour ... What Goes with What ... Fool-Proof Combinations

3 Using Colour with Flair All Around You 71
Decorating in Your Palette ... Increasing Colour Confidence ... Patterned for Success ... Eliminating Expensive Mistakes ... Climbing the Wrong-Coloured Walls ... Importance of Lighting ... Themes & Schemes

4 Men and Colour   86
Men and Hair Colour ... Suiting yourself ...
Living With Colour

Part II   *What Colour Says About You*

5 Using Colour to Influence Others   92
Yang or Yin? ... Colours for Job Interviews ...
Communicating with Colour ... Power Colours

6 Your 'Shady' Past and 'Brilliant' Future   105
The Colour Profile Quiz: What Do Your Colour
Preferences Mean? ... Likes, Dislikes and
Secret Desires ... Conclusion

Bibliography   122

Index   123

The Colourtime Quiz

Which Colourtime Are You? Are you Sunrise, Sunlight, or Sunset?

I call this system the 'Colour Clock,' because everything in nature, including colour, works on a time clock. We associate certain shadings, tints, values, and intensities with specific times of day.

Answer the following questions without stopping to analyze your responses. Your answers should reflect your immediate reaction to colour.

Question 1.

Look at the three palettes on the opposite page. Which one do you like most? Don't choose it on the basis of one particular colour, or the colours that you think are most popular now.

Choose the one you really like best. Get a sense of the whole picture and how the colours look together.

Circle one: Sunrise   Sunlight   Sunset

Question 2.

If you could completely redecorate your home, which palette has most of the colours you would choose?

Circle one: Sunrise   Sunlight   Sunset

Question 3.

If you could buy an entirely new wardrobe, which palette has most of the colours you would choose to wear?

Circle one: Sunrise   Sunlight   Sunset

Question 4.

Look at yourself in a mirror, near natural light if possible. Then answer the following questions to determine your personal colouring. Make the best selections you can from the choices given, or ask a friend to help you. Mark your answers and tally the results.

What colour are your eyes?

Blue

Blue, clear light blue or medium blue Sapphire blue Blue, but almost grey	Sunrise
Blue with a little grey Peacock blue	Sunset
Blue, but I don't see myself distinctly in either of the above categories	Sunlight

Brown

Dark, rosy cocoa brown – light medium or dark Very dark brown, almost jet black	Sunrise
Amber Warm golden brown – light, medium or dark Very dark brown	Sunset
Brown, but I don't see myself distinctly in any one of the above categories	Sunlight

Hazel

Grey hazel, a combination of blue, grey, and perhaps some green	Sunrise
Golden hazel, a combination of brown, gold, green and perhaps some blue	Sunset
Hazel, but I don't see myself distinctly in either of the above categories because I have many colours in my eyes	Sunlight

Green

Bright blue-green Bright green with some yellow undertones	Sunrise
Greyed blue-green Green gold Green grey	Sunset
Light or medium blue-green, but I don't see myself as being distinctly in any of the above categories	Sunlight

Sunrise (A.M.) Colour Samples

Sunlight (Midday) Colour Samples

Sunset (P.M.) Colour Samples

Plate A

What is your hair colour?

(If you colour your hair, answer this question by giving your youthful natural hair colour.)

Blonde

Ash blonde – light, medium or dark Platinum blonde Towhead	Sunrise
Golden or coppery blonde – light, medium or dark	Sunset
Blonde – light, medium or dark – but I don't see myself as being any of the above. I think I have a mixture of the blondes, both warm and cool tones together	Sunlight

Red

Auburn, with cool blue undertones Strawberry red	Sunrise
Golden copper red – light, medium or dark Rust-wine red, like bordeaux	Sunset
Red, but I think I have a combination of both warm and cool tones	Sunlight

Brown

Ash brown – light, medium or dark, but without gold Dark brown, may have auburn highlights	Sunrise
Golden brown – light, medium or dark – sometimes with copper highlights	Sunset
Brown – light, medium or dark – but I don't see myself clearly in any of the above categories. I have both warm and cool tones mixed together	Sunlight

Black

Blue-black	Sunrise
Brown-black	Sunset

Grey

Snow white Silver grey, with cool blue undertones	Sunrise
Cream white Winter white Pewter grey (not as blue grey as silver)	Sunset
Grey, but I don't see myself as being distinctly in any of the above categories. I'm a mixture	Sunlight

What is your skin tone?

(Often people are unsure of their precise skin tone. If you have difficulty answering this question, don't worry. Just pick the answer that you think comes closest to describing your colouring.)

Olive

Olive with green undertones	Sunrise
Olive with warm golden undertones	Sunset
Olive, light, but I don't think I belong in either of the above categories	Sunlight

Black or Brown

Blue-black Rosey brown	Sunrise
Golden honey brown (light, medium, or dark)	Sunset
Very light brown	Sunlight

Fair

Fair, cool, white	Sunrise
Warm, creamy white	Sunset
Ivory	Sunlight

Beige

Rose beige Rose pink	Sunrise
Warm peach beige (light, medium, or deep)	Sunset
Beige, but I have a mixture of both rose and peach tones	Sunlight

Colour Wheel

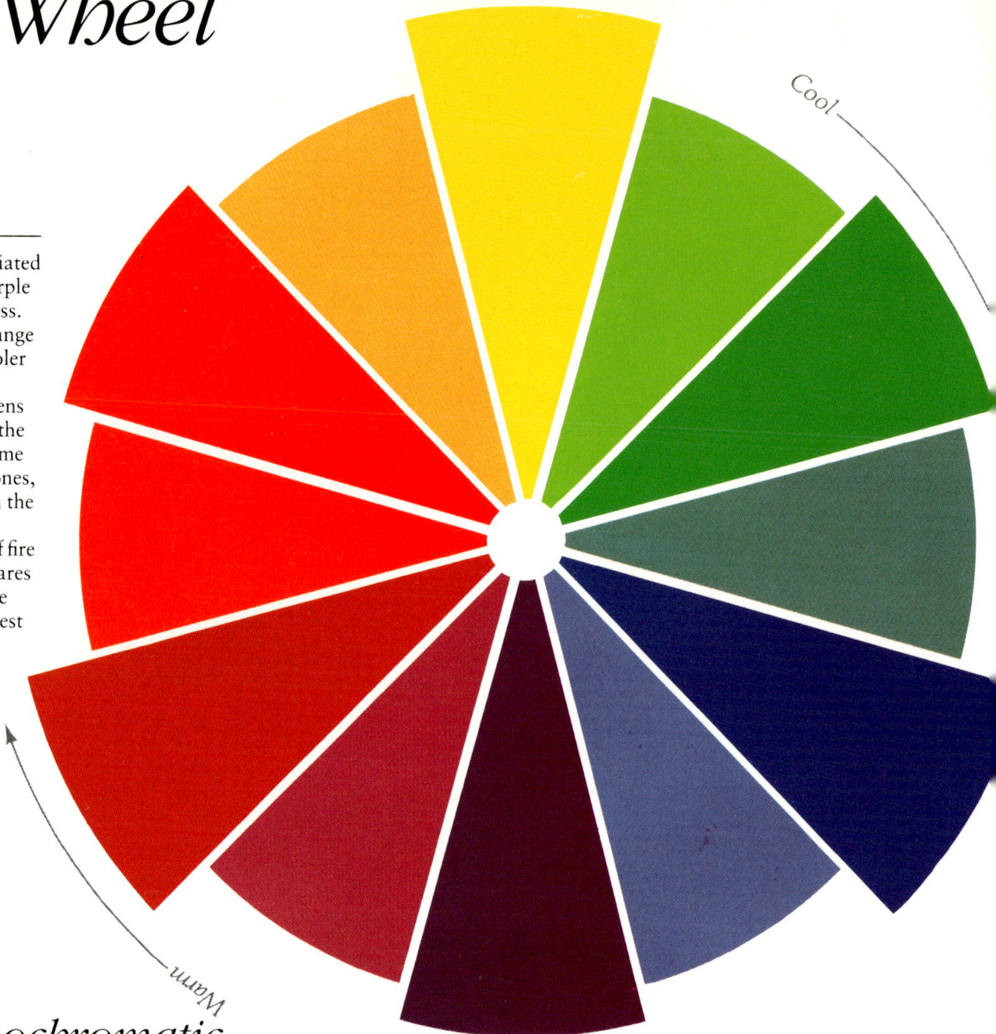

Warm and Cool Colours

Red, yellow, and orange, are associated with warmth. Blue, green, and purple (violet) are associated with coolness. But changing an undertone can change the temperature. Blue-reds are cooler than yellow-reds. The redder the purple, the hotter it gets. Blue-greens are cool, but the closer to yellow, the warmer green gets. Every colourtime palette has both warm and cool tones, but Sunrise glistens primarily with the coolness of water and air; Sunset radiates mainly with the warmth of fire and earth. The Sunlight palette shares the subtle shadings of both. See the Colourtime palettes to find your best warm and cool colours.

Monochromatic

This scheme uses just one hue in varying shades or tints – for example, a Sunrise bright turquoise, aquamarine, and aqua; or shocking and shell pinks from the same palette.

Analogous *(Related)*

These colours adjoin each other on the wheel. They are safe to use together because they are closely related, such as warm reds, oranges, and yellow. To expand your family, add a touch of the adjoining yellow-green. For example: the multi-coloured Sunset combination of Geranium, Apricot, Terra Cotta, Gold and Honey, accented with a touch of Dill. Vary your shadings and allow one colour to dominate.

Complementary *(Contrasting)*

These are the colours which lie directly opposite to each other on the wheel. They intensify each other. Strong contrasts scream for attention. Lightening or deepening one or both of those hues can be subtly pleasing, as in the Sunlight palette combination of Peach Melba and China Blue.

Plate B

Score your answers to Question 4

My eye colour is	☐ Sunrise	☐ Sunset	☐ Sunlight
My hair colour is	☐ Sunrise	☐ Sunset	☐ Sunlight
My skin tone is	☐ Sunrise	☐ Sunset	☐ Sunlight

If you marked two or three in one column, this is definitely yours. If you marked one in each colourtime, go with Sunlight. Sunlight is a balanced combination of both Sunrise and Sunset, so it's a no-fail compromise. You may decide later that you have an emotional attachment to one palette or another, and change your mind. But more about this later. Stick to Sunlight for now.

Quiz Explanation

After analyzing the preferences of thousands of students, clients, and audiences, I know that the colourtime that people choose in question 1 is likely to be the one they also choose in questions 3 and 4. Most people will discover that the colourtime palette that contains their skin, hair, and eye colour is their preferred palette. They will often, but not always, choose that same colourtime palette for their surroundings. Your natural colour sense draws you to those colours.

You are part of nature's design. A misused hair tint can cause a hair colour mistake, but you can't fool Mother Nature. You are born with blending skin, hair, and eye colour. Everything in nature is designed to blend.

Study the colour of Siamese cats and you will see how their eyes, fur, noses, and foot pads all blend into a particular colourtime. Look at Irish setter puppies in a pet store window — all of their golden colours fit into the Sunset palette.

Go back to question 4 to make certain that you chose the best colours. Check your eye colour first in a good light. You may discover colours in your eyes you've never seen before. Brown-eyed people are often amazed when I point out the green in their eyes. Look at the undertones in your skin and hair. Take the time to really study yourself.

If you find it hard to be objective, ask a friend to help you. It's often easier when someone else helps you judge your colouring. If two out of the three personal colourings, such as your eyes and hair, are in one of the palettes, you can feel assured that it is your palette. If you colour your hair, try to find your natural hair colour on the list. Many times clients tell me that they can't remember — it's been so long since they've seen it! Ask an old friend or your hairdresser, if he or she is the only one who knows 'for sure'.

Look at the clothes in your wardrobe. Since one assumes, you do most of the choosing, most of the colours will be in your colourtime. The colours in your home are a less accurate indication of your colourtime because other people are often involved in your choices, or because you had to work with colours that were already there when you moved in, such as carpeting or tile. But if you did the decorating and are really happy with your choices, the colours that you chose can also help you find your colourtime.

If, however, you are not happy with your choices in either your clothing or your home, or you're just ready for a change, the following discussion can help you determine which colourtime to use.

Where Your Choices Take You

If you circled the same colourtime palette in answer to all four questions, you should have little trouble choosing colours because you have a really strong affinity for the particular colourtime palette that you circled. You will feel your absolute best when you wear and are surrounded by the colours in that colourtime. That's the good news.

The bad news is that because you have this strong pull in one direction, you might be somewhat inflexible in decisions involving someone in another colourtime (husband, wife, business partner, teenaged daughter, others involved in planning a wedding, etc.).

You are not, however, apt to be confused about your colourtime. People are likely to ask for your advice because you are so decisive – but you're likely to advise them to use *your* favourite colours!

We are most likely to choose our clothing colours from the same palette that contains our skin, hair, and eye colours. But if the palette you circled for question 2, about the colours you would choose for your home is different from the other palettes, you could be content to 'dress' your surroundings in a different colourtime than the one in which you dress yourself.

Your clothing should reflect your personal colouring, but your home may reflect a particular mood from another colourtime. We'll get into those moods later. You are more flexible than the person mentioned earlier who has chosen the same palette throughout, but the bad news here is that you may have difficulty making a decision because you are so flexible.

Is it possible to favour two colourtime palettes equally? The answer to that question is yes. You could probably be happy using any of the colourtime palettes you circled. In terms of decorating, your choices give you more freedom to convey different moods. You might choose to do a bedroom in the Sunlight palette, and the kitchen in the Sunset palette, for example, and perhaps a child's room in the Sunrise palette.

You are probably delightful to work with because of your flexibility, but may find it hard to decide which palette to use and where. Extra freedom of choice can mean extra confusion!

I often advise clients to go with their hearts and not with their heads. The colour that gives you that emotional tug is the one you want to use. If you analyze and agonize too much, you lose the point of what colour is all about.

With clothing choices, I feel it's best to choose the colourtime palette that contains your personal skin, hair, and eye colouring and stay with it most of the time – it's more flattering and makes you look your best. It is also more practical, easier on the budget, and everything you wear will blend well with other colours in the same colourtime. If, however, you have a really favourite colour in another colourtime, there are ways to integrate that colour into your wardrobe. We'll get into that later.

If you have a strong aversion to a particular colourtime, then you obviously should avoid using it because it will make you uncomfortable to be surrounded by that palette. You are also likely to be definite about your other dislikes. This shouldn't become a problem unless you're living with or sharing an office with someone who absolutely loves that colourtime. There are compromises, which we will also explore later.

Have you ever been given a jumper from someone in a colour that you felt looked awful on you? Chances are that it was in the giver's colourtime – not yours. They may have spent hours knitting it and think it's just wonderful. You can begin to solve that problem by telling everyone what your colourtime colours are – they may take the hint the next time they give you something.

Should you experiment with a colourtime that you didn't circle? Chances are that you won't want to, but trends do tempt you, your lifestyle may change, and your moods definitely do, so that you feel the need to try something totally different. And unless you live alone, you also have other people to consider.

My experience has been that you will tire more quickly of colours that are not included in your preferred colourtime as indicated by the quiz. It's risky to experiment in a large area when you're investing a lot of money.

Try these colours instead in the family room, a second bathroom, or on your verandah – some fun place where you can change colours inexpensively with a coat or two of paint, should you decide later that those trendy colours aren't really you at all.

Try a different colourtime in an inexpensive piece of clothing or accessory before you invest a whole on something that may turn out to be a mistake.

Did you circle all of the colourtimes for all of the answers? You are the kind of person who says 'I love all colours!' That sounds wonderful and you're very flexible – but somewhat fickle and definitely moody!

Just like a kid in a corner shop, you may want 'two of those,' and 'three of these,' and, wait a minute – another 'one of those.' Some of my wildest (but most fun) clients say they like *everything*. And they *want* everything... sometimes all in the same room or in the same outfit.

If this sounds like you, there are three ways for you to avoid becoming totally uncoordinated.

1. In clothing, go with the palette that contains your personal colouring, for the most flattering and organized solution. If you still feel that you want to wear all three palettes, don't combine them all in one outfit. It does mean that you will have three separate wardrobe palettes, each of which needs blending accessories and, if you're a woman, blending makeup colours.

2. In a home, use all colourtimes, but use each in a different area. The result may be a house of many moods, but you probably have the personality to handle it!

3. Use the Sunlight colourtime palette because it overlaps into both the Sunrise and Sunset palettes and offers you a wide, but more subtle, range of choices.

If you're having difficulty finding your own colouring in one particular palette, or you simply cannot decide which pleases you the most, then I suggest that you also go with the Sunlight colourtime. This palette is a happy compromise and because your own colouring is likely to be so varied that it is difficult for you to see which palette is yours, you may belong right in the middle with the Sunlight palette.

Do colourtime choices ever change? In some people they do, in others they stay constant over a lifetime? Your colouring may change as you age. Your hair may start to grey and soften your look. Your skin may (but not always) start to pick up more yellow with age. (Think of handsome lace or cotton – not old newspapers!)

Your eyes do fade, but that can be an advantage because the undertones then begin to come through and you can introduce these colourings into your wardrobe.

You may have been born a Sunrise and loved many of this palette's bright shades as a child and young adult. But as nature ages and softens your colouring, you might want to switch to the softer Sunlight palette. Then again, your colouring may remain fairly constant, especially if you colour your hair, and you may continue to wear the same colours you wore when you were younger.

Elizabeth Taylor will always look wonderful in Sunrise colours. The vivid contrasts of her dark hair, light skin, and violet eyes will continue to allow her to wear accents of brilliant colours, or the stark contrast of black and white. **Cary Grant's** hair went from darkest dark to whitest white, but the same blue-wine ties are as elegant on him today as they were in his old movies. **Lucille Ball** is an eternal Sunset. Can you imagine that inimitable redhead ever going grey?

Don't let the existence of many different types of colouring in each colourtime confuse you. There are light, medium and dark colourings in each palette. All you need to do is to look at the closest description of hair, skin, and eyes in each colourtime list to come up with the right combination for you.

Dynasty's **Linda Evans** has cool, ash blonde hair, rose-beige skin, and grey-blue eyes. **Lynda Carter** has blue-black hair, fair-rose skin, and clear light blue eyes. Both women are combinations of the Sunrise palette and wear many of the same colours beautifully. My clients are often amazed to see how individuals with colouring that appears to be so different on the surface can actually wear many of the same colours.

Oriental skins may fall into any of the three colourtimes. Some Asians have very blue-black hair and eyes, with the cool green olive undertones of Sunrise; others have the deep but very warm hair and eye colouring and warm olive skin of Sunset. If you are of mixed racial background, you may fall into the Sunlight palette.

Ruddy or florid skins may also be found in all three palettes, so basing your choice on hair and eye colour may be the best way to find out which palette is yours. For example, a florid skin may typically be found in redheads, or redheads who have gone grey. If their eyes and hair have warm undertones, even though the skin is flushed, they will be in the Sunset palette.

Let your initial, emotional, reaction to the three palettes be your guide, if you are in doubt, and you will find yourself in your best colourtime.

Choices - 'Right' or 'Wrong'

It is important to remember that there are no 'right' or 'wrong' answers to any quiz in this book. No one is going to give you a bad mark and make you stand in a colourless corner if you make the 'wrong' choices.

You cannot make a mistake in choosing your colourtime palette, because colourtime choices are simply a question of personal, natural reactions. I am not placing you in a little colour cubicle and asking you not to stray from it.

When I do seminars, classes, or conventions, for example, I take three large collages with me, one in each colourtime. I ask for volunteers to stand in front of the chart they prefer. It is interesting to me that children have no problem at all in doing this; they are so free and uninhibited. But adults become very analytical and self-conscious and often choose colours because of what a friend in the audience suggests. Your friend – wonderful person that he or she may be – cannot tell you how you feel or what you see. You may have been surprised by your response to the quiz. Did you find yourself in a palette you would never have expected to be in? That should tell you something. Maybe it's time for a change.

Part I

What Colour Can Do For You

Chapter 1

Discover the Secrets of The Colour Clock

What is the Colour Clock?

I call this system the 'Colour Clock,' because everything in nature, including colour, works on a time clock. We associate certain shadings, tints, values, and intensities with specific times of day.

Writers and poets traditionally use colours to describe various hours. Dawn is apt to be 'cold and grey.' Sunshine is invariably yellow. And cowboys always ride off into a 'blazing golden sunset'. The Impressionist painters transformed art history with their efforts to capture the full impression of nature and the play of light on a particular scene at a particular time. Impressionist Claude Monet, renowned for his studies of water lilies, often painted the same subject to show how its colours varied at different times of the day.

Colours do appear to vary during the course of a day because of changing light and the presence of various particles that float around in the atmosphere.

The Colourtime Palettes

In the earliest hours of the day, warm colour begins to emerge from the cold, grey dawn. A rosy glow appears before the dazzling sun actually begins its ascent. Because sunrise is sunset in reverse, the shadings progress from the darkness of blue and grey to purpled rose-mauves to the splendor of the red-orange glow. But because the atmosphere is generally cleaner and more moist

17

in the morning, the colours of sunrise are much less fiery than those of sunset. This dewy 'wetness' permeates the Sunrise colourtime.

Occasionally, when the air is very clean, there is a clear green streak across the sky just after the dawn breaks. Later in the morning, the sun changes into a brilliant yellow-white. Blues are brightest in the early hours and the sky is at its clearest.

An undertone of cool blue pervades most of the Sunrise (AM) colourtime.

In the afternoon, you see the Sunset (PM) colours. As the number of yellowed dust particles in the atmosphere increases at this time of day, most colours appear to take on a golden hazy, or mellow quality. Colours appear 'drier' than they do in the morning.

In the late afternoon, as the sun goes down, you see the fiery shades of sunset. Gold is the pervading undertone of sunset's orange, rust, warm reds, and curried greens. At dusk, the spectral rays of deep blue take over, often combining with the reflected reds to become a red-violet glow.

In the very middle of the clock, between 10 a.m. and 2 p.m., is the Sunlight (Midday) colourtime palette. The intensity of the sun is greatest during these hours. Even when the sun is covered by clouds, the force of its reflected light remains strong. Any object that receives direct sunlight during these hours seems slightly diminished, because intense light dazzles the eye and makes the colours appear somewhat muted.

Since this colourtime is derived from both the AM and PM palettes, it offers the widest range of choices, but the colours are subtle – they never scream. This is the palette of pleasing, luscious pastels of every hue. Any of the tints may be deepened to a darker value for contrast.

> Charcoal, black, and navy blue represent the shades of night and pre-dawn when all colours are shrouded in darkness. They may be used with all of the colourtime palettes. They are part of 'Nature's Crossover Colours' and are explained more fully later in this chapter. The crossover colours are part of every palette.

As the sun travels around the clock, you see that every colour in the spectrum is represented throughout the daytime hours. Mother Nature does not exclude any colour from any segment of the clock. She simply varies the undertones, intensities, and values in each colourtime palette.

Let's go to the Colourtime Quiz to find out about your natural harmonies. The quiz helped you identify your colourtime preference. Now you'll find the colours that belong in each colourtime.

Which Colourtime Are You...
        SUNRISE   SUNLIGHT   SUNSET ?

Using Sunrise (A.M.) Colours

These fashion illustrations show you how the colours of the sunrise palette can work to create wonderful wardrobe with sparkling style. The combinations you see are all drawn from the palette on the adjoining page.

Some interior designers use renderings (a detailed sketch) to show a client how a projected colour and design scheme will work. Stan Taylor, A.S.I.D., of Hollywood uses the Colour Clock to help his clients feel comfortable and happy in their homes. At right Stan has used colours drawn from the Sunrise (A.M.) palette.

Fashion Illustration: Sharon Adams Interior Illustration: Stan Taylor, A.S.I.D.

Plate C

Sunrise Palette A.M.

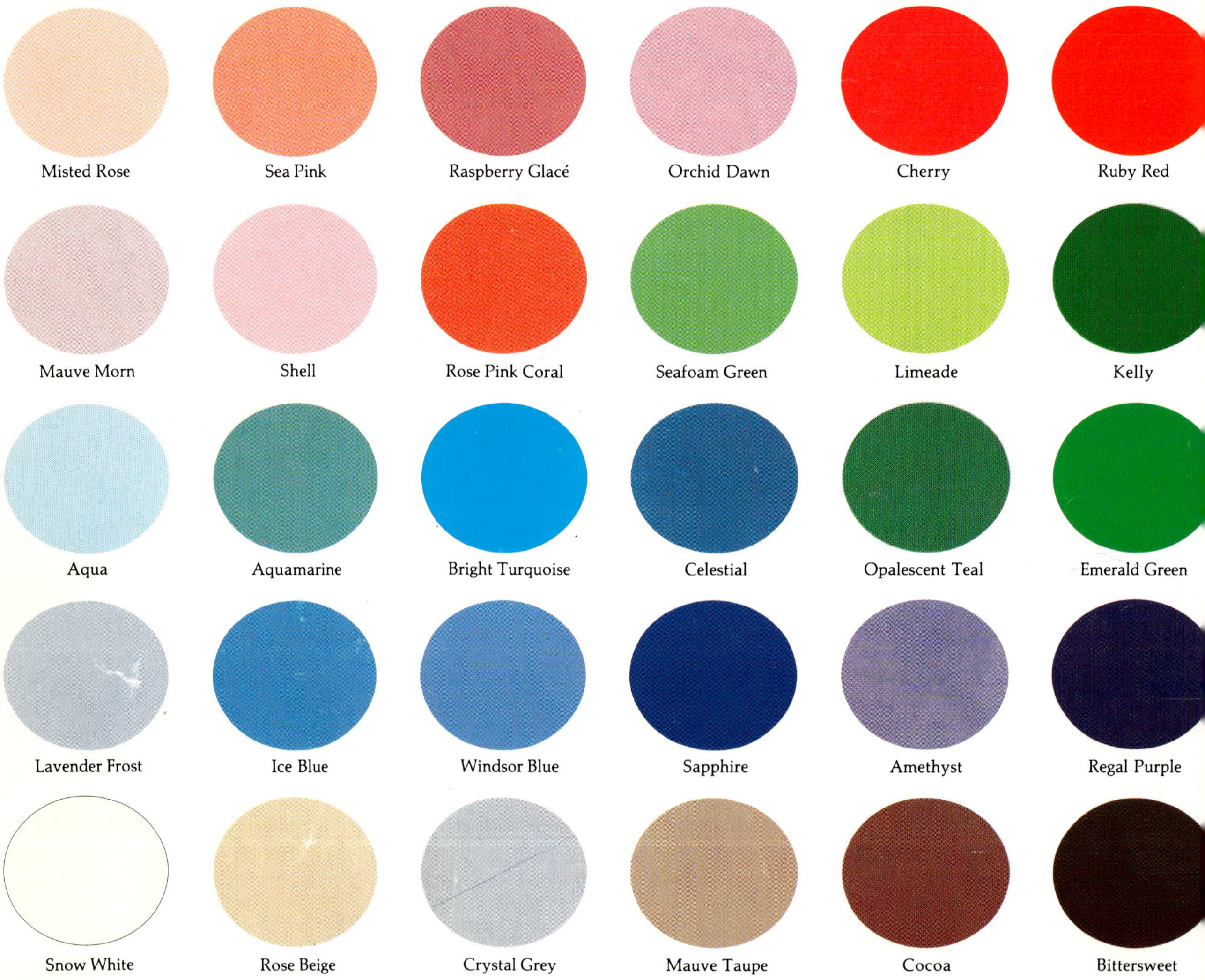

Daffodil	Daybreak	Fuchsia	Shocking Pink	Watermelon		
Misted Rose	Sea Pink	Raspberry Glacé	Orchid Dawn	Cherry	Ruby Red	
Mauve Morn	Shell	Rose Pink Coral	Seafoam Green	Limeade	Kelly	
Aqua	Aquamarine	Bright Turquoise	Celestial	Opalescent Teal	Emerald Green	
Lavender Frost	Ice Blue	Windsor Blue	Sapphire	Amethyst	Regal Purple	
Snow White	Rose Beige	Crystal Grey	Mauve Taupe	Cocoa	Bittersweet	

The Crossover Colours:
All colourtimes can use these colours because they are nature's most versatile.

Plate D

The Sunrise (AM) Colourtime Palette

If you chose the Sunrise palette for your clothing and/or interiors, the natural elements of water and air are a strong influence on the predominantly cool blue undertones of your colourtime palette. The illustration shows samples of those colours.

Your palette literally sparkles, and many of your colours are such 'jewel' and 'royal' tones as:

Amethyst	Sapphire Blue
Opalescent Teal	Ruby Red
Regal Purple	Emerald Green
Bright Turquoise	Windsor Blue
Aquamarine	Fuchsia

The cool colours are often transparent and frosty:

Ice Blue	Crystal Grey
Snow White	Lavender Frost
Aqua	Celestial Blue
Seafoam Green	Orchid Dawn
Mauve Morn	

The warm colours in your palette are pure and cooled down:

Shell Pink	Watermelon
Rose-Pink Coral	Sea Pink
Raspberry Glace	Misted Rose
Cherry Red	Shocking Pink

The kelly and lime greens of your palette are fresh, clean and bright, as are daffodil and daybreak yellows.

Orange and red-orange play a very small role in your colourtime and are usually least favoured by people choosing this palette. Use them sparingly as accents, just as nature does in the short time span of sunrise. Oranges will work best for you when you lighten them to rosy pink-corals or deepen them to rich cocoa and bittersweet browns.

Grey, rose-beige, and mauve-taupe are natural neutrals for your palette.

Your best white is pure white.

Famous people who share your Sunrise colourtime are:

Elizabeth Taylor	Paul Newman
Princess Diana	Linda Evans
Cary Grant	Mel Gibson
Liza Minelli	Debbie Newsome
Simon Gallaher	Jeanie Little

The Sunset (PM) Colourtime Palette

Did you circle the Sunset Colourtime for your clothing and/or room settings? If you did, you prefer the Sunset (PM) Colourtime palette. The natural elements of fire and earth are a strong influence on the predominantly golden undertones of your colourtime.

Your palette is primarily warm and is often described as 'earthy.' The warm, spicy shades are important to you.

Cinnamon	Paprika

But you should not be so 'down-to-earth' that you do not enjoy a touch of the exotic:

Curry	Avocado

These greens can give special flavour to your life:

Bay Leaf	Dill

Your taste can also be tempted with the sweet shades of:

Honey	Apricot
Peach	

Other earth colours that are important to this Colourtime are:

Brick Red	Terra Cotta
Bronze	Camel
Bordeaux	Harvest Gold

Your light to medium pinks are best when they are dusty and warm, like ash rose and coral dust.

In addition to the spice greens, hunter, warm taupe, and khaki are basic to your colourtime. The fiery portion of the Sunset palette is reflected in tomato-red, red-purple, burnt orange, geranium, and hazy magenta.

Your cool colours are the mellowed:

Heathered Purple	Deep Teal
Lilac Dusk	Peacock
Dusk Blue	Antique Turquoise
Cadet Blue	Smoke Grey
Deep Periwinkle	

The colours you should use most sparingly are strong shocking pinks. Mother Nature uses these hues in brief splashes, and so should you.

Your best white is cream.

Examples of famous 'Sunset people' include:

Victoria Principal	Lynda Stoner
Maggie Taberer	Telly Savalas
Bryan Brown	Robert Redford
Jane Fonda	Fleur Fenster
Barbra Streisand	

The Sunlight (Midday) Colourtime Palette

Did you circle Sunlight for your clothing and/or interiors? If you did, your preference is for the Sunlight (Midday) colourtime palette.

This colourtime dips into both Sunrise and Sunset. Yours are the softened, muted, sun-drenched tints. They are more intense than pale pastels, never 'wishy-washy' or nondescript.

Any of the natural elements of air, water, fire, and earth are present in your palette, but they are never flamboyant. The hot shades of Sunset would overwhelm this palette, but dusty rose is perfect. The sapphire blue of Sunrise would work better if gentled to the muted tones of Limoges.

The tints and shadings are the delicious ice cream, sherbet, and confection colours. This is the fattening palette. A ice cream parlour would be a perfect place to check you your best colours, but if you are dieting, try a fruit stand instead.

Your warm shades are truly delectable:

Peach Melba	Lemonade
Buttercream	Strawberry Cream
Melon	Raspberry Sherbet
Banana	Bisque
Mocha	Creme Caramel

The colours of the plates on which you serve your food describe some of your best blues:

    Wedgwood   Delft
    China   Limoges

Your other cool shades are subtle and interesting:

    Grape   Creme de Menthe
    Plum Cordial   Soft Turquoise
    Orchid   Teal
    Mauve   Celadon
    Jade   Wisteria
    Lilac

Your greens include a sprinkle of Mint and Sage.

Because your colours are gathered from both the AM and PM palettes, you can express yourself especially well with such variegated combinations as neutral tweeds with small flecks of colours, subtle checks, or plaids. Avoid really bright colours; they won't work as well for you and are best used as an added touch.

Subtle is a key word for Midday palettes. If given a choice, opt for the subtle. True red is the best of the brights for Midday, but avoid using it in neon intensities. Fiery orange is not a good choice for this palette. Lighten it to orange blossom or deepen it to chestnut, and you will be much happier with it.

Any of your colours may be deepened in value. You may prefer evergreen to creme de menthe, or wine to mauve when the occasion calls for a little more dignity or sophistication.

Neutral taupes such as sand, bark, and mushroom, and dove greys combine well with both the warm and the cool hues of your colourtime, and since neutrals are never noisy, they will also work best for you.

Your best white is vanilla – not too pure and not too creamy. 'Almost' whites with pastel undertones are also good.

Examples of famous 'Sunlight' colourtime people include:

    Candice Bergen   Daryl Somers
    Olivia Newton-John   Lee Remick
    Bob Hawke   Katharine Hepburn
    Prince Charles

The Crossovers

Certain colours on the Colour Clock are called crossover colours. Because these colours occur most frequently in nature, your eye is accustomed to seeing them in combination with many other colours.

The crossovers may be used with all of the colourtime palettes. They're often used as background colours, either in combination with other colours, or in the same way a neutral colour might be used.

Sky Blue

Did you ever look at a red geranium, a purple iris, or a yellow daffodil against the backdrop of a blue sky and think 'What an awful colour combination… Mother Nature got it wrong!' Of course not. We're aware of the blue of the sky around us nearly every day. Blue skies far outnumber cloudy (or smoggy) days in most climates. As a result, our eyes and minds are accustomed to a blue backdrop for nature's myriad colours.

How can you take advantage of Mother Nature's favourite background colour? Hang a painting with lots of blue sky as background in a room done in any of the three palettes. Not only will it not intrude, it can be an excellent way to bring a cool touch into a warm room for colour balance.

Evergreen

Would you banish a fern from your living room because it clashed with the lounge suite?! When nature 'arranges' flowers, green is the one colour that appears in virtually every composition. Nature's greens are among the most versatile of hues, particularly shades of grass green, leaf green, forest green, and evergreen. When we're outdoors we're surrounded by green plants, trees, shrubs, and grass.

Sunlight Yellow

The clear yellow of sunlight permeates our atmosphere. Sunlight yellow works well as a neutral colour. It is a good colour to bring into a room done in cool colours, to give a touch of warmth. Sunlight yellow is shared by all colourtime palettes.

Brown (Terre Brun)

The French call a certain brown 'terre brun.' The phrase sounds more elegant than 'dirt brown,' doesn't it? Yet dirt brown – the brown of the soil – is what it means. The varying earth tones associated with soil, tree bark, and woody plants are an integral part of nature's basic colour scheme. Your eye is accustomed to these unobstrusive colours, which function marvellously well as neutral colours.

The term dirt brown is more likely to evoke thoughts of muddy dogs than beautiful flowers unless you're a gardening enthusiast who knows the potential for lush growth inherent in dark, rich soil. It's a brown that is difficult to describe as either warm or cool because it's a happy marriage of both undertones. But other browns and beiges have a decided warm or cool cast and look best when combined with colours in a particular colourtime. They are shown with each palette in the colour section.

Raisin
This is a very popular shade of brown. It is slightly purpled – the colour of the fruit from which it is derived – and blends beautifully with all colourtime palettes.

Aubergine
Aubergine is the French word for eggplant. Their adroit use of this deep purpled-maroon, especially in interior design, has made it a classic.

Deep Wine
The various names for this dignified basic, darkest of the reds are often confusing; many of them are used interchangeably, and the colours of the wines themselves vary widely.

> The deep, rich sample shown with the crossover colours is the most versatile wine and flatters all colourtime palettes.

Taupe (Greige)
This is the ideal neutral. 'Fawn,' 'otter,' and 'mushroom' are often used to describe taupe. It combines beige and grey, and, as a result, blends well with all palettes. Some taupes have a light yellow-green undertone and work best with the warm colours of each palette. Other taupes have a mauve undertone and work well with cool colours. The straight grey-beige colour called 'greige' is the most versatile neutral. 'Sand' is often the name given to the lightest taupes.

Black
Black is the inevitable colour. No matter what colours we are exposed to during the day, we are ultimately exposed to the black of night. Black is the ultimate in sophistication and spans all colourtime palettes.

Grey
Grey appears as the first light of early dawn, often as an undertone to the blue skies of daylight, and adds depth to the deeper blue of dusk. When the sky is not blue, it is usually grey, and since grey days are less cheery than blue days, we often feel the need to add a touch of vivid colour to grey to give it pizazz. Grey runs the gamut from almost black to nearly white. Pearl grey, grey flannel, and charcoal work with every palette.

Navy
Dark navy blue is sometimes referred to as midnight blue. It is associated with black and the colour of night. It is a familiar background colour and the most universal of all basic colours.

True Red
This is the red that has both cool and warm undertones. It works well for all palettes, but needs to be deepened or used as an accent in the Midday palette.

What Colour Can Do For You

Colour is an essential ingredient in the enhancement of your environment. It can direct and divert the eye, communicate emotion, create moods and optical illusions, delight, or dignify. It has enormous influence in your life, starting from the day you were first able to discern the colours in the world around you.

Nature's paintbox yields wonderful possibilities. There are limitless tints or tones to exite you or calm you, elate you or depress you, warm you or cool you. Colour may heighten your awareness and make you more sensitive to your surroundings.

Colour can enhance your self-image and make you feel marvellous. I have seen some amazing changes after having helped clients find their personal palettes. One of the first messages you give to other people before you ever say a word is 'spoken' in the colours you use. Haven't you walked into someone's home and instantly felt warm and comfortable or known you were going to like a person even before you met? You were responding to the universal silent language of colour.

An 'Eye' For Colour

Is an 'eye' for colour like an 'ear' for music? Are we born with a sense of colour? I think both of these questions can be answered 'yes' and 'no.' Some experts feel that we may be predisposed to certain abilities through artistic ancestors, whereas others believe an 'eye' for colour is acquired through the learning process.

You don't have to be born a child prodigy to play the piano. Through instruction and practice you can learn to play well enough to satisfy your needs. You may never perform like Billy Joel or the late Arthur Rubinstein, but you can still get a sense of satisfaction and enjoyment out of playing.

The same holds true for colour. You may not have been born with artistic ability, but you can learn how to use colour so that it will work wonders for you and give you tremendous satisfaction. When you arrange flowers in a vase, take a photograph, or serve food on a plate, you are the artist.

What You See

You have a natural affinity for or attraction to certain colours and colour-times. When you walk by a flower shop and see many beautiful arrangements, one or two will catch your eye. There may be a big selection to choose from, but some are more special to you than others. Texture, scent, and design will also attract you, but colour often draws your attention first.

What you see pleases your aesthetic sense — your appreciation of beauty. Some of the bouquets are so special to you that they almost take your breath away. You are attracted to certain colours because they are in tune with your natural colourtime preferences.

Decorating magazines are full of handsome rooms, but some beckon to you more than others. Some seem so comfortable to you that you wish you could climb right into the picture. There is an almost irresistible influence that tugs at you and appeals to your emotions.

One of my clients, Kay S., redecorates every few years, invariably in beiges and browns. She felt that she was in a colour rut, but explained that those colours just felt so natural to her. When we got into a discussion about that particular combination, we discovered that her school uniform had been beige and brown. Several clients have turned away from the colours that they had to wear for years (such as army fatigue green), but Kay had pleasant memories — she adored her school years, remembering them as the happiest time of her life. She was a good student who felt a sense of accomplishment and was secure and popular. I told her that if browns and beiges made her feel all of those good things, she should continue to use them.

Many people make the mistake of switching to 'new' colours simply because of the novelty. They soon grow tired of their selections and realize they never felt quite comfortable in that environment.

If the same colours continue to make you happy over the years, there's no need to switch. Often a touch of an interesting accent colour is all that is necessary for a new look. In Kay's case, I suggested touches of teal and tomato from her PM colourtime palette to add a little pizazz.

Colour Your Thinking

At this point, you may be thinking, 'If I have this natural affinity, why is it that I may not be happy with my colour choices?' There are several explanations:

1. You allow too many outside influences to colour your thinking (pun intended). These can include family, friends, fads, persuasive advertising, and the bargains you find so hard to resist. Bargains may be marvellous for the budget, but the bargain that sits forgotten in the wardrobe is no bargain. Have you ever chosen carpeting and hated it from the moment it was nailed to the floor? Or tried a bathroom wallpaper and felt that you had contracted instant yellow jaundice when you saw it reflected next to your face in the mirror? Chances are that the colour you chose (or that someone else chose for you) was not in your personal colourtime.

Do you often give people gifts in the colours you like best? They probably do the same to you! With the Colour Clock method, you can let everyone know what your colourtime is, and learn to choose colours that will please everyone on your gift list. This will save you money by helping you avoid expensive mistakes.

2. Colours are rarely used in isolation. Choosing one colour that you really like may be simple for you. But combining that hue with other shades, tints, and intensitives can be troublesome. Don't let finding the correct combination deadlock your efforts. If this is the part that confuses you, read on. The 'how to's' and how they work follow in the next chapter.

3. The psychological and emotional impacts of colour can delight you or devastate you. It is almost impossible to separate the 'seeing' of colour from the 'feeling' because so much of what you see is based on what you feel. Colours evoke emotions – some pleasant, some very unpleasant. You can turn off a terrific colour because of some experience long past.

Do pink roses make you think of the first corsage you ever got (or gave), or do they remind you of the time that you ate too much fairy floss at a carnival and got sick on the way home? Your reaction to a particular colour will definitely be influenced by your personal experience.

Certain colours and colour combinations can put that wondrous tape recorder in your head on 'instant rewind.' You never really forget anything you have ever learned. You just deposit it in your memory bank for future withdrawals.

Using Sunlight (Midday) Colours

These fashion illustrations show you how the colours of the Sunlight palette can create a wardrobe with versatility and creative style. The combinations you see here are drawn from the palette on the adjoining page.

Stan Taylor, A.S.I.D., rendered this colour sketch, at right, of a room in the Sunlight palette. Midday colours are often the happy compromise for people with differing colour tastes in the same household, since this palette uses subtle combinations gathered from both the A.M. and P.M. palettes.

Sunlight Palette Midday

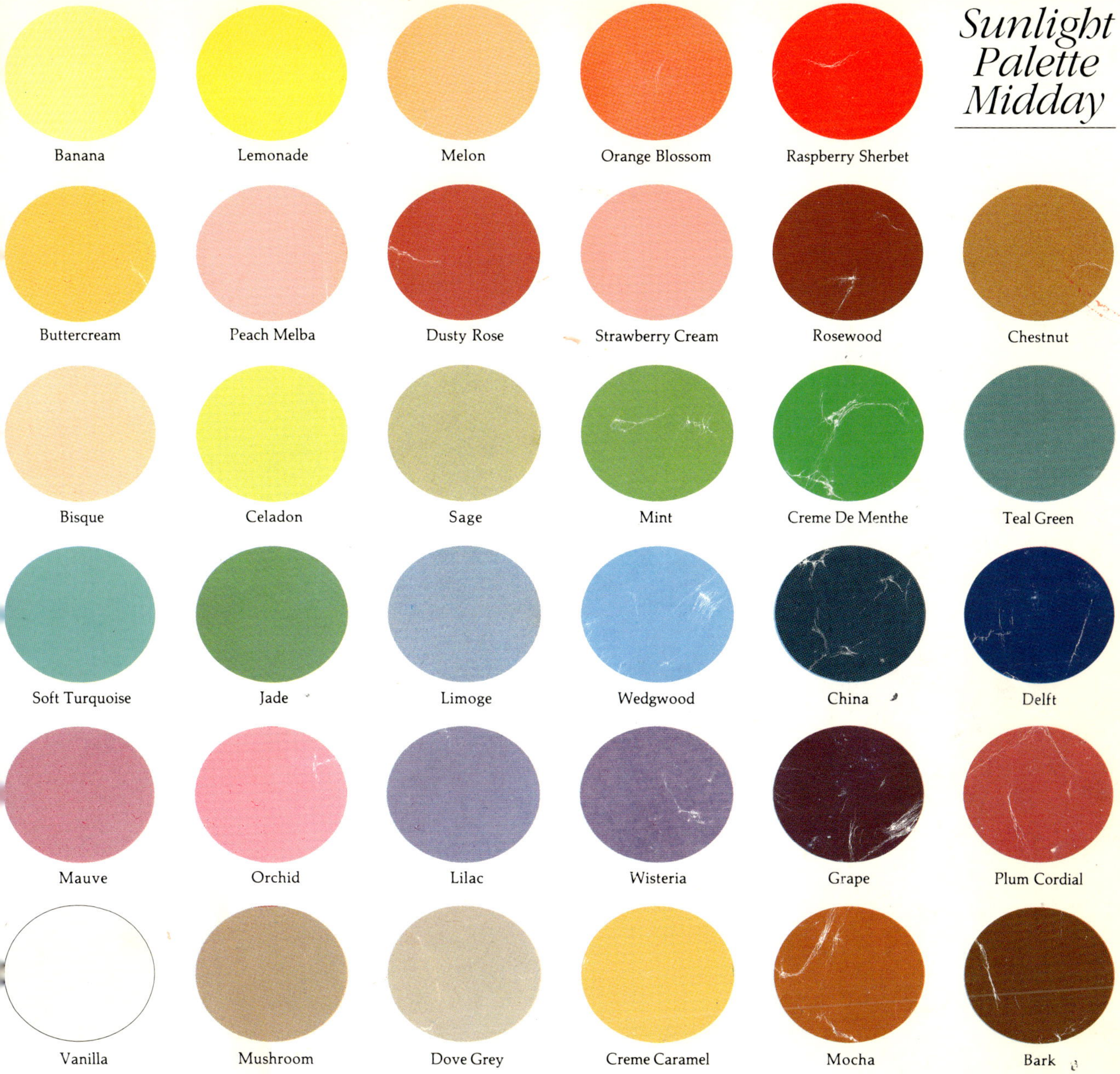

Banana	Lemonade	Melon	Orange Blossom	Raspberry Sherbet	
Buttercream	Peach Melba	Dusty Rose	Strawberry Cream	Rosewood	Chestnut
Bisque	Celadon	Sage	Mint	Creme De Menthe	Teal Green
Soft Turquoise	Jade	Limoge	Wedgwood	China	Delft
Mauve	Orchid	Lilac	Wisteria	Grape	Plum Cordial
Vanilla	Mushroom	Dove Grey	Creme Caramel	Mocha	Bark

The Crossover Colours:
All colourtimes can use these colours because they are nature's most versatile.

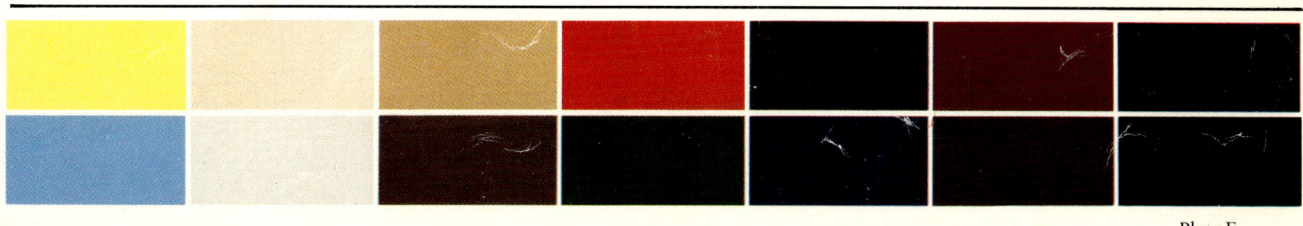

Plate F

Keeping an Open Mind

Even though you may respond favourably to most colours in your colourtime, you may not like every single colour because of a previous negative experience you associate with that particular shade. Most of the time you can't even remember what the memory is. Consider the following story:

Martha L. came to me for a colour consultation because her husband told her he was sick of her decorating with the 'same old nondescript neutrals' and wanted some purples in the house. That instantly told me that her husband was highly creative and unusual. Men rarely like purples for decorating, especially in the lighter values, but this one turned out to be an artist and a very interesting person.

She, however, had a really hard time with anything remotely purple – any shade, including, and most particularly, lavender. I asked Martha to try to remember why she might be having such a difficult time. She thought about it for several days and then called with this story:

As a child, she had a wonderful loving relationship with her grandmother. The little girl would bring sprigs of lavender to her, since it was her grandmother's favourite colour. The grandmother had beautiful Sunrise silver hair and wore the colour a great deal. She also loved touches of lavender throughout the house in delicate potpourris.

When my client was eight, her beloved grandmother died. Of course, she was buried in a lavender dress and everyone sent various shades of purple flowers to the funeral. Interestingly, some funeral homes did (and still do) decorate in purples, since in some cultures it is considered a mourning colour. A purple wreath was often placed on the front door.

We had all the clues we needed to realize why Martha was so turned off by those colours. It had been her first experience with death and she was so traumatized by it that she simply locked the painful event away in her subsconcious. The memories of that difficult day faded but her grandmother's favourite colour had become associated in Martha's mind with a deep sense of loss.

When my client asked my help in overcoming her purple prejudice, I gave her the same advice I give to anyone who really wants to become open to trying new colours: For every negative experience, find a positive flip side of pleasurable associations. In this particular case, once the client had remembered the unpleasant associations, she could deal with them and turn to the happier aspects.

There is a delightful P.S. to this story. For her daughter's wedding, the mother of the bride chose – you guessed it – a lavender dress. When I called to congratulate her on her daughter's marriage, she thanked me profusely for opening her up to purple. Now when she looks in the bedroom mirror and sees herself surrounded by the lavender accents, she realizes how much like her grandmother she has become (her AM palette is the same), and what marvellous stories she will be able to tell her own grandchildren.

If she hadn't allowed herself to experience the colour, those important years with her grandmother might have remained hidden forever. Few of us have such poignant stores to relate, but we all need to keep an open mind to colour. You never know when you might unwrap a box of memories – all in living colour.

Ambiance

Each palette expresses a different mood. The French have a word for this (they usually do). They call it ambiance. Your answers to the quiz tell you, by looking back at the colourtime you circled for question 2, where you will feel most in harmony with your surroundings. If you circled more than one colourtime, simply choose the palette that best expresses the mood or ambiance you want to convey.

An environment done in the Sunrise colourtime palette conveys a soothing and refreshing message, perfect for a summer porch filled with wicker or a place at the beach.

Sunset colours convey warmth and security. They are perfect for 'lived-in' rooms such as a country kitchen, a den, a family room – ideally, a room with a fireplace.

Environments done in the Sunlight (Midday) colourtime palette are inviting, easy to live with, and never overwhelming. The delicious ripe-fruit colours are often used in dining rooms and fine restaurants. They make a perfect compromise for people who share an environment but have differing colour tastes. We explore this subject further in Chapter Three, 'Using Colour With Flair All Around You.'

Remember that each colourtime palette has both warm and cool colours, plus light, medium, and dark values of each of them, so there is enormous flexibility within each palette. If you have a really strong affinity for a certain colourtime, you never have to leave it.

For example: if you're a strong PM person who chooses to do your house in the warm range of sunset colours, but want some cool tranquility in the bathrooms, you simply dip into the cool PM colours. These deep teals, antique turquoises, and greyed-blues are not as pure as the AM cools, but they will still impart a cool feeding, and you will find them far easier to live with than the AM blues and greens. And, as I mentioned before, you will be less likely to tire of your colourtime cools because they relate so well to the other colours in your PM palette.

This is equally true for each of the colourtime palettes. You can stay completely within the framework of your own colourtime and still achieve the necessary variety. As a matter of fact, it's important to maintain a balance between warm and cool colours, regardless of the colourtime you have selected.

> If only cool colours are used in any one area, the mood can be chilling. To be complimented on the cool, serene ambiance of your house is one thing, but to be told that it seems cold would definitely not be a compliment!

Always observe this fundamental guideline: Cool colours should be balanced by a touch of warmth and warm colours by a touch of coolness. If you were to use only bright, warm colours in a room, that room could start to feel uncomfortably hot – especially in summer.

In a warm room, your eye will search for something cool for balance. In a cool room, your eye searches for a touch of warmth. But don't carry your balancing act too far – a combination of half-warm and half-cool simply doesn't work. It is far more aesthetically pleasing to keep the cool colours dominant and the warm colours subordinate, or vice-versa. The rewards will be felt each time you enter that room.

Walter Scott, the renowned 20th Century-Fox set designer who has won many awards over the years, told me an intriguing story about an ambiance he created for **Barbra Streisand.** He was doing the sets for the film version of *Hello Dolly* and being the delightfully considerate man that he is, wanted to be sure that Barbra felt comfortable in her portable dressing rooms. He discovered that one of her favourite colours is a lovely dusty ash rose called 'Bois de Rose.'

He did the entire area in variations of that colour, complete with leaded glass, creamy antique lace curtains, and accents of topaz, another Streisand favourite. He knew that Barbra loves Art Nouveau shadings and by combining the film's turn-of-the-century setting with 'her' colours was able to keep the *Hello Dolly* mood alive for her both on and off camera. Barbra loved it. She is a strong PM person.

In her spacious New York apartment, she combined the ash rose and greyed-blues of her colourtime in the formal living room. The library is a deep bordeaux accented with bronze accessories. Her bedroom is done in a deep lilac haze, rust, and evergreen. These highly unusual, interesting, and dramatic combinations reflect Barbra's individuality, creativity, and personal colourtime. She feels very much at home there – just as you will feel when you are surrounded with the hues of your preferred colourtime palette.

Walter is a definite AM individual. He does research in a den with mauve-taupe walls, where there is little to distract him from his work. Its ceiling is sky blue. When he needs to reflect on a thought, he tells me, he just looks up and is refreshed.

For contrast, and to relieve monotony, he uses sparkling red and yellow accents in pillows and paintings. He also uses Mexican tin and touches of shiny lacquer – two textures that are very complementary to an AM setting.

Come vacation time, Walter escapes to the water. Nothing is more restful and serene to him than to be surrounded by blue. Morning is his favourite time of day. There really is no question about the colourtime that best mirrors his preferences.

Think of a place you don't like to visit and you'll probably come up with the dentist's office. One of my clients is a dentist whose motto is 'gentle dentistry.' How could we use anything else but the gentle, Midday colourtime palette for her? We decided on soft mauve and powdered blues with wine carpeting. Even the equipment is done in soft, non-threatening colours. Soothing colours can be crucial in this sort of stressful environment. Calm patient and relaxed doctor equal gentle dentistry.

You may not think you're aware of colour, but you truly are. The message may be subliminal, but it's always there to create an effect and to colour your decisions, your moods, and your world.

Intimate Environments

Of the many environments that surround you, that of your clothing and cosmetics is the most personal. It is called your 'intimate environment.' You choose clothing and cosmetic colours just as you do anything else in your environment – because you have an affinity for those colours and because they create a pleasing and comfortable atmosphere around you.

Your aesthetic colour sense – what you see – plays an important role in your wardrobe decisions, especially in terms of what you see in the mirror. If you have hair the colour of burnished copper, one glance in the looking glass tells you how smashing you look in bronzes and peaches. And if your skin is sallow, no one should have to tell you to avoid chartreuse.

You may have really good 'instincts' about your personal colours. You have learned how to read the reactions of others and you know when your choices are validated by a favourable comment – or no comment at all. After years of working with people and their colour needs I have found that the eye really doesn't lie about flattering or unflattering personal colours. Let your Colourtime Quiz be your guide. If you have any doubts at all, choose your clothing colours from the colourtime that contains the colours of your skin, eyes, and hair. You will feel best when you look your best, and you will look your best when you feel your best... it is a completed circle.

One of the most compelling reasons for doing your wardrobe in your preferred colourtime is that all of your clothing will blend and harmonize.

The major portion of your personal environment extends to the world around you – your home and all of its furnishings, your office or place of business, your garden, your car. Colour choices are of obvious importance because your extended environment is a reflection of you.

You want to be sure of these choices because they involve some of the biggest investments you will ever make. The Colour Clock will give you the confidence to overcome old prejudices and open your mind to exciting new possibilities.

Understanding Undertones

To better understand the differences in the colourtime palettes, think in terms of undertone. There are both warm and cool colours in all three palettes. Warm AM colours have an undertone of the rosy glow of sunrise. Warm PM colours have an undertone of the gold of sunset. The Midday colourtime dips into both palettes, but never with a heavy hand.,

For greatest harmony, colours blend best if they are in the same colourtime palette. For example: shocking pink has a definite blue undertone (AM). Apricot is a light warm yellow-orange (PM). Shocking pink and apricot would not be a particularly pleasing combination because they are not in harmony. Paprika and apricot are more effective together, because they have the same yellow-gold undertones. They are both PM colours.

Cool AM colours are often 'sharper' than PM colours. Imagine the electric blue-green of a tropic ocean in the morning. These are AM colours. Now picture the deeper blue of the ocean at dusk. You are now seeing PM colours. Next imagine that ocean at high noon. It is still a beautiful blue-green, but because of the sun's intensity, it appears a bit muted.

Another example of pleasing combinations from the same colourtime palette is AM ruby with shell pink. If a third colour were chosen to harmonize and you wanted to use a neutral tone, rose-beige would be the most effective because of its similar undertone.

Geranium and brick red are handsome PM colours. A blending neutral would be cream beige. A Midday combination of grape, mauve, and mushroom would be striking, yet subtle.

Purple, which blends red and blue, is a complex colour. Redder, warmer purples blend best with the Sunset colourtime. Cooler, bluer purples blend best with Sunrise. Lighter and deeper tones blend best with Sunlight colourtime. It can be difficult to see how much red – or blue – undertone is in a particular purple.

If you're having 'purple' trouble, use your colour palette. If your palette is elsewhere, your eye will have to be your guide. If the colour you're combining the purple with pleases your eye, go with it. Another trick for shopping when you don't have your palette with you is to compare similar colours. If you hold one purple against another (or compare any two similar colours), the undertone will pop right out at you. It's always best, of course, to try to keep your swatches with you, to be on the safe side.

Teal is a wonderfully versatile shade that flatters many skin types by bringing out the pink or peach of the skin. It is also a complex blend; some teals are bluer, and some are greener. Check your colour swatches to see which teal works best with the palette you are using.

If you love a colour that doesn't appear in your favourite colourtime, try it in a light-reflective fabric. The colour will change according to the way the light either bounces off of it, or is absorbed by it, creating 'hills and valleys' of variation. It will be more flattering than the same colour would be in a dull, matte finish.

Mixing Palettes

As a general rule, colours from the Sunrise palette blend best when used together and colours from the Sunset blend best when used together. However, as with any rule, there is always the exception. The opposing Sunrise and Sunset palettes may be used together for deliberate discord or as attention-getters. This is a common technique in advertising, packaging, sign painting, and billboards.

You will often see colourtime palettes combined in wallcoverings, furnishings, and carpeting in model homes. The reason for this is to make the house so memorable that long after you have forgotten how dramatic (or hideous) the combinations were, the home and location will stand out in your mind as something to remember.

If the effect is blaring, like the psychedelics of the 60's, it is called 'discordant.' Do you remember AM kelly green used with PM hot purple? If the effect is not hard on the eyes, it is called a 'hybrid' combination. Cool AM purples and warm PM rusts are examples of hybrids that many designers have combined well, especially in intricate paisley prints.

Many combinations in the Sunlight colourtime are examples of interesting, but subtle, hybrid blends. The Sunlight palette shares peach with the Sunset palette and mauve with the Sunrise palette. When used together, the unique combination of peach melba and mauve is very flattering to the mixtures found in the Sunlight colourtime. They quietly claim your attention, but the more discordant mixtures of the Sunrise and Sunset palettes command it.

The illustrations show you some of the most attractive combinations in your colourtime. Use them to help guide you in making your choices.

If you have an especially strong affinity for a particular colourtime, you might be perfectly content never to leave it. And you may choose not to. But if you have an especially favourite colour, and it's not in your preferred colourtime palette, I would be the last person to advise you *never* to use it – never is a long, long time. It might evoke some wonderful childhood memory. If you always chose lemon gumdrops over every other flavour, you will remember the colour as well as the taste. Lemon yellow brings back memories of delicious trips to the neighborhood shop or a Saturday afternoon at the movies with your best friend.

If lemon yellow is not a part of your colourtime palette, scatter a bit of that colour through a room via accents or touches. You should always have a dish full of lemon gumdrops on hand to keep those happy memories alive – and maybe to create some special ones for *your* children to cherish!

The key to mixing colourtime palettes successfully is to keep one palette dominant and the other subordinate. The dominant colourtime palette should be 75 percent (or more) of the combination, and the subordinate colourtime should be 25 percent (or less). You may vary this somewhat. Try 85 percent or 90 percent dominant. You'll find these proportions also work well. This system works for any combination involving two colours, even if they come from the same colourtime.

Just as with music, discord is not always unpleasant, but our ears may tire of too much discordant sound. The same principle applies to colour. You may deliberately combine colourtime palettes, but don't forget to do your maths. Your eyes will tire of too much vibrant discord. And if your eyes get tired, you get tired, grumpy, and unsettled, and start looking for a change.

I have suggested that clients who want to experiment with a wild and crazy combination that equally combines two opposing palettes buy a beach towel or a pair of shorts. If you get tired of it, you haven't invested a fortune. But if you have gone to the expense of putting up new wallpaper and want to claw it off in three months, you're in trouble. Be careful when you decorate. Choose combinations that you can live with for a long time. Most of us simply can't afford the time, energy, or money to keep changing.

The most effective use of combined palettes I've ever seen was in the charming Georgetown home of a friend of mine in Washington, D.C. Helen M. was widowed at an early age. Her husband had been with the State Department, and they had travelled all over the world. She collected fabulous furnishings and had exquisite taste.

Helen loved the AM colours. She had a beautiful Oriental rug and she decorated her living room around it. The carpet's colours were wine, an off-white with a blue-pink undertone, and cool brown; distinctive touches of peacock blue shimmered throughout the design.

The walls were painted the same pinkish-white of the rug; Helen's marvelous antiques were of highly polished mahogany and cherry; and the luxurious velvet couches echoed the rug's wine tones. Small touches of peacock blue appeared on two tiny provincial chairs by a bay window, and in the needlepoint and Persian tapestry pillows that graces the sofas.

The room was done predominantly in the AM palette. But Helen told me that she always had to have a touch of that wonderful PM peacock blue in every room of the house. The first time she showed me a picture of her husband, I knew exactly where her love of that colour came from. Mr. M. had a kindly face, with the most iridescent greyed blue-green eyes I have ever seen. She will always associate that colour with the happy years of her marriage.

Exploding Old Myths — White Does Not Go With Everything

Pure white is not a neutral colour. It is dazzling and brilliant and impossible to ignore. It will not 'go with everything.' For decorating purposes, it is often necessary to add a touch of another shade or tint as an undertone to white paint to cut the glare that white generates. In an office or work environment, it is extremely important to control glare to reduce eye strain. Off-white is a more effective neutral.

Because it is so highly reflective, especially in a fabric with a sheen, pristine white acts as a mirror as it reflects the colour used immediately next to it. For example, if you use orange checks on a white background, the white will warm up slightly, because the orange is so warm. Bright colours are slightly dulled next to pure white.

Mixing whites never works. Off-whites will look dull and dingy next to pure white. Your beautiful antique lace curtains will look yellowed and faded next to a snow-white lamp shade. Super-sheer white fabrics, such as scrim curtains, disclose the colour behind them, so they appear less white than a heavier texture would.

The AM colourtime palette can use pure whites better than the PM or Midday, but a bit of blue-pink, light blue, or grey as an undertone would help to reduce glare.

In a Midday environment, a bit of any pastel, depending on the other colours in the room, makes a good undertone to white.

If you are using PM colours in the room, it would be best to add a tiny bit of yellow, gold, or beige, depending on the depth of the shade desired. This would give a slightly creamy cast and would blend best with the other PM colours.

White reflects into adjacent areas, which makes it excellent to use near darkened spaces. Pure white enlarges any area in which it is used so when decorating your bed or your body, remember that anything amply upholstered will look larger in white!

Frank Westmore, of the famous family of make up artists, told me that he discovered the enlarging effect of pure white when he was working on the film, *Geisha Girl,* with **Shirley MacLaine.** He used the traditional white makeup and, as he put it, 'Shirley's face looked like the moon!' In order to 'save face,' he added a bit of pink as an undertone to the stark white, which visually reduced the size of her face so that she no longer looked distorted. One of Japan's leading cosmetic houses now uses Frank's formula.

In clothing, a white sheer or semi-sheer fabric becomes an off-white. The undertone of the skin comes through and mutes the whiteness somewhat, making it a better choice for midday or PM skin tones. AM skin wears pure white best.

The glare from a white shirt or blouse can make the face look pale. Women can compensate for this by wearing more makeup, unless they have very pink, very dark, or very olive skin, which provides good contrast to white in the AM palette. If you love pure white, and you have a Midday or PM skin tone, save it for summer when your skin is tanned. Many of my clients in those colourtimes tell me they only wear white in summer, when the tan of the skin reflects into the white and makes it more becoming. If you're a Midday or PM with dark skin, you can wear pure white year round, but cream white or vanilla will blend best with the other shades of your palette.

Pure white is also at its best at night, when there are softening shadows. For Midday and PM men, crossover sky blue, light yellow, sand, and light grey are usually more flattering than pure white shirts. The AM skin may also wear those tints, since they are crossovers.

Regardless of fashion's whims, pure white stockings look too stark. A subtle sand is better. As for men – save your white socks for the tennis court.

Kay Sazarin, dynamic Hollywood hair colouring expert, travels all over the

Using Sunset (P.M.) Colours

These fashion illustrations show you how the colours of the Sunset palette can work to create a terrific wardrobe with excitement and flair. The combinations you see are drawn from the palette on the adjoining page.

This detailed sketch, or rendering, at right, was done by Hollywood interior designer, Stan Taylor. Stan frequently uses the same sketch in different colourtimes to show clients the different moods colour creates. Here he has used a combination of colours from the Sunset (P.M.) colourtime palette.

Plate G

Sunset Palette P.M.

Harvest Gold	Honey	Burnt Orange	Geranium	Tomato
Apricot	Peach	Coral Dust	Ash Rose	Brick Red	Bordeaux
Curry	Khaki	Bay Leaf	Dill	Hunter	Avocado
Dusk Blue	Cadet Blue	Deep Periwinkle	Antique Turquoise	Peacock	Deep Teal Green
Smoke Grey	Warm Taupe	Magenta Haze	Horizon Purple	Lilac Dusk	Purple Heather
Cream White	Camel	Terra Cotta	Cinnamon	Paprika	Bronze

The Crossover Colours:
All colourtimes can use these colours because they are nature's most versatile.

Plate H

world demonstrating colouring techniques. She loves to wear dazzling white on stage because it is so luminous and attention-getting. These qualities give pure white preferred status with many performers. But if you have PM colouring, as Kay does, dramatize your makeup and add colour to your face so that you won't look pale or sallow when you wear white.

Magenta Haze - blue, white, touch of red
Horizon Purple - blue, white, yellow, touch of red, touch of black
Lilac Dust - white touch of red, touch of blue
Camel - white, touch of yellow
Cadet blue - white, touch of blue
Dusk blue - white, blue, touch of black
Aubergine - blue, white, yellow, red + black
Purple Heather - blue, red, touch of white

terre brun - ~~french~~ cardigan goes w. dusk blue trousers + brown belt
~~deep wine~~ - trousers
Lees wine
~~Horizon Purple~~ - cardigan

celadon jacket w. black
Navy = black or Charcoal
Dark Grey = bright emerald (co-ord) dirty apple (Khaki)
Dove Grey = lemon (co-ord)
Bright Pink (Schiaparelli pink)
(Cardinal - purple heather)
Bright Turquoise goes with navy.
Blue Red - tweed
Tds) Pale Yellow goes w. cold grey (dirty ivory)
Dirty Ivory (Dove Grey) - trousers
ds - Bright Turquoise looks good w. white + pale green (summer)
(winter) w. horizon purple

37

Chapter 2

Making The Colour Clock Tick For You

Putting Colours Together Successfully

One of the greatest challenges of working with colour is to combine colours effectively and attractively. Choosing a single colour to use is much easier than deciding what goes with what.

Most of the old colour rules have disappeared. Using blues with greens was once considered in terrible taste, and combining red with pink was a no-no. The only rule today is 'Never say Never.' Think in terms of guidelines rather than rules, which can hamper your creativity and take the fun out of being open to new ideas. Guidelines can give you the confidence to know how – and what – to combine.

The simplest and safest way to combine colours is to stay within the borders of the colourtime you have chosen to use. The formulas that professional designers use can provide you with the 'know-how.' Mastering them can help you to create terrific combinations.

All colour formulas are based on the colour wheel (see Plate B). The Colour Clock is designed to help you make happy marriages between harmonious and compatible colours. Of the many guidelines for colour coordination, here are the least complicated:

Harmonious Relations

All colours are derived from the primary hues of red, yellow and blue. If you mix equal parts of two of these primaries, you get the secondary colours of orange, green, and purple. They are colour kin. Orange is the child of yellow and red. Purple results from the union of red and blue. Each of the secondary colours has a harmonious relationship with its 'parent' colours.

If you use green, yellow, and blue together (or orange, yellow, and red, or purple, red and blue), you have what is called a related or analogous colour scheme.

The colour wheel shows you the colours that are most closely related; these provide some of the easiest colour schemes to work with. They are also the least apt to offend. These schemes are based on adjacent colours – yellow, yellow-orange, orange, and orange-red, for example, which share the same undertone.

> If you want to expand your colour 'family,' you can add a cousin from either the yellow-green side or the red side.
>
> When you add these extra colours to clothing choices, they're best kept within the confines of a print; if used as separate colours, the relatives may get a little noisy as they vie for attention.
>
> It is difficult to make a mistake with rooms done in related colours whose undertones are in the same colourtime. If you want to be a bit more daring, try an expanded analogous combination. Rooms done in these colours occasionally need areas of solid black, white, or grey for definition, or a touch of pattern to avoid monotony.

Thank You For The Complement

Complementary or contrasting colours are those directly across from each other on the standard colour wheel. They are called complements because they complete each other. Green, for example, is the complement to red, and never looks greener than when it is next to red. Conversely, red appears reddest when next to green. A red rose seems even redder against a green leaf.

Orange complements blue, and yellow complements purple. I was finally convinced that **Elizabeth Taylor** actually does have violet eyes when I saw her at the Academy Awards in bright daffodil yellow chiffon. When used in the brightest intensities, complementary colours are instant 'zing' and can be real show-stoppers. The complementary colour effect is a major reason for advising redheads to wear green.

Complementary combinations can be super-dramatic, but can also be strident in their call for attention. People with outgoing personalities often love them. When designers package products, they frequently use the brightest intensities of complementary colours. On your next trip to the supermarket, look at the brilliant array of detergent boxes all begging for your attention. Notice how many are done in the sharpest complementary combinations.

Complementaries can be used to wonderful advantage, but can also boomerang. If your skin flushes easily and you have a ruddy complexion, bright green next to your face will bring out the pink (light red) in your skin. The green should be lightened or deepened for a more flattering effect. When the intensity of one or both of the complementaries is muted, the combination is much easier on the eyes. For example, a shocking AM pink and deep emerald green combination is less jarring optically than the same shocking pink when paired with kelly green.

It is best to stay within your colourtime when using complementaries so that your eye will not tire of combinations quickly. If you do combine palettes, use only a touch of the subordinate colourtime. Remember our dominance and subordination guideline: one colour is always the star and takes centre stage, while the other is the supporting player.

For example: In a PM room of paprika and hunter green, the walls and mini-blinds might be hunter green with accents of lighter green in plants and accessories. The area rug, chair pads, and place mats are paprika against a warm pine dining table and chairs. Green is the dominant colour, paprika the subordinate. (The pine set is treated as a neutral because it is unobtrusive, but its warmth blends with the PM colours.)

When intense or strongly contrasting colours are offset by neutral colours, the combination becomes much richer. The neutrals enhance the brighter colours by making them easier to view. For example: Vivid AM orchid dawn and daybreak yellow might be great fun in a Hawaiian print shirt, but when these hues are subtly mixed with grey, taupe, or beige, the combination gains both elegance and a quiet neutral shade to use as an accessory colour.

What To Do If Your Chair (Or Hair) Is Fading

As you follow the circle of the colour wheel, think of your own colouring. Complementary colours in your colourtime can help to keep you from fading away, (as we all do to some extent with age). Blue eyes are enhanced by browns, raisins, oranges, and corals. Green eyes are flattered by wines, pinks, and reds. Hazel eyes are chameleons that pick up and reflect many of the colours that are worn near them. They often combine many colours, but one colour usually predominates. Complementary colours are very effective with hazel eyes and can virtually change their colour.

Brown eyes and hair are complemented by greens, especially blue-greens. Since grey is a neutral, it really doesn't have a complementary colour as such, but it is enhanced by touches of colour. Neither does black have a true complement, but both bright hues and white contrast effectively with it.

If you are blonde, purples shades and tints will make you look blonder. As we have noted, green is often suggested for redheads, but bright blues are actually more complementary because 'red' hair is closer to orange than to red.

Complementary colours can be used very effectively in interiors. A large painting with blue sky in the background can be a perfect foil for the coppery carpet of a PM room. Wallpaper laced with leafy greens may be just the antidote to the tired pink tiles and plumfing fixtures of a once-bright AM bathroom.

If your AM blue chair is fading in a bright, sunny room, a pillow with a touch of orange – but just a touch – may restore its vitality. In a Midday room, soften the orange to melon. If your celadon chair is disappointingly dull, use something around it, on it, or under it that contains red, rose, or wine, and watch it come alive. If you are using the Midday palette, the softer complementaries will be more pleasing.

Monochromatics

A monochromatic colour scheme uses only one hue in varying shades and tints. The secret of a successful monochromatic scheme is to select all of the variations of this single hue from the same colourtime in order to avoid clashing undertones.

If you are working with varying shades of AM blue-red, for example, those from seashell pink to ruby red look best together because they have the same blue undertone. A good PM red combination would be brick red with honeyed corals. An attractive Midday combination would be dusty rose and strawberry cream.

Weddings are excellent occasions for being creative with monochromatic colour schemes. The mother of the bride can be lovely in varying tones of an AM aquamarine with undertones from the same colourtime. When I coordinate wedding parties, I often suggest that everyone wear monochromatic colours from the same colourtime. It's much easier to choose flowers, the wedding pictures are lovely because everyone's colours blend so well, and a beautiful occasion becomes even more beautiful.

In monochromatic colour schemes, light and bright shades and tints draw the eye first. So unless you want your feet to be the focal point, use darker colours at the lower part of your body and lighter and brighter shades as you move toward your face, which then becomes the focal point.

In the case of the bride's mother, who plans to wear aquamarine crepe with an overlay of chiffon, the aqua tones of the top of the dress would gradually deepen towards the hem. Her shoes would be a slightly deeper shade than the hem. If she chose to wear a flower in her hair, it should be as light as, or lighter, than the top of her dress. Darkening the colours at the lower part of the body gives stability to the figure, makes it appear slimmer, and directs attention to the face.

The ultimate monochromatic colour scheme uses only one colour with very little variation. The effect can be quite stark or even severe, but it is very dramatic. Using a variety of textures and shapes can help to avoid too much sameness.

I recently received a call for help from a woman who had done her apartment's entire living/dining area in beige. The contemporary room was well done and quite comfortable, but she was starved for colour. Rather than interrupt the wonderful lines of the furniture and the flow of the room — and because she lived in a mild climate — I suggested that she keep banks of colourful potted plants and flowers on the balcony, which could be seen through the sliding glass doors.

Most of her furniture faces the balcony and she simply changes the pots with the seasons to whatever flowers in her favourite colourtime are then in bloom. At night, spotlights illuminate the greenery and she feels as though she lives in a garden, even though she is in the heart of a big city.

Duochromatics

A duochromatic combination consists of just two colours. There are also two basic guidelines to remember here: The first is that the eye will be drawn to the area where the two colours meet. A dark bathing suit may make your figure appear smaller, but it will also draw attention to the upper thigh, where the light colour of the skin meets the dark of the suit, or vice-versa. If you are chunkier than you'd like to be, a bathing suit that matches your skin tone is more flattering because it blends with your body and presents no line of demarcation to draw the eye.

The second guideline again focuses on the basic maths of one dominant and one subordinate color — 75 percent or slightly more of one shade and 25 percent or less of another.

These proportions are less distracting than equal divisions of colour. For example: A navy suit with red shoes, red bag, red sweater, and red hat would be much too busy. The eye is drawn to too many areas at once and you don't know where to look first.

A better choice would be to make the suit, since it already covers so much area, the dominant colour. The shoes should be navy, the bag could be navy with red trim. The sweater could stay red, but the hat would be better in patterned combination of navy and red. Attention would then be brought to the face, making it the focal point.

The effectiveness of duochromatics can be in the simplicity of combining just two colours. Just as with monochromatics, one or both of the colours may vary in value or intensity. For example: Crossover shades of dark and light grey, used with aubergine and a touch of mauve, would be considered a duochromatic combination, but would offer more variety than straight grey and aubergine with no variations. Complementary combinations could also be considered duochromatic, but are only those that oppose each other on the colour wheel.

A duochromatic combination may be very dramatic in its simplicity. A traditional example is black and white. Black is a crossover colour. If you are a stickler for precision, blue-black is specifically AM, umber black is PM, and the Midday is a combination of both. But it is splitting hairs to try to differentiate between them and I never suggest that my clients run around searching for just the right black.

Finding similar undertones in black only becomes important when you are combining blacks in the same outfit. We've all had the experience of putting a black shirt with black pants only to discover that the blacks looked awful together. They were from different colourtimes.

It is less critical to match blacks in a room setting than it is in clothing. In interiors, you are apt to use a variety of textures together and colours and textures are more widely spaced than they are in clothing. The best combinations of black and white are black and pure white for AM; black and cream white for PM; and black and vanilla for Midday.

Simple, unadorned, stark black can be fabulous in clothing whenever it provides strong contrast, such as on redheads, blondes, or silver- or white-haired wearers in any colourtime. It is also wonderful on fair or rosy AM skin, light creamy PM skin, and the ivory skin of Midday. For the rest of us, black needs a touch of pizazz near the face, such as a hint of red in a patterned tie, or the contrast of a light or brightly coloured shirt.

Trichromatics

A trichromatic colour scheme uses three colours. One colour dominates (approximately 70 percent), the second is subordinate (20 percent), and the third is used as just a touch (10 percent). This third colour can be used effectively to draw the eye to a given area, making it a focal point. If you were cooking, you'd call it a 'pinch.'

> If a duochromatic room has become a bit tired, adding a third colour for accent is a good way to revitalize it. A living room done in PM deep teal and dusk blue could be perked up with coral dust pillows. An accent colour should be used more than must once — you might repeat the coral dust as emphasis in a print or in some other accessory piece.
>
> When dressing in classic grey flannel and pearl, such as in a suit with a shirt, wine is an excellent highlighting accent — as in a wine and two-tone grey scarf or tie.

By placing the third colour in the scarf or tie, you draw attention to the face. If you were to add this accent in a belt, the waist becomes the focal point. Use the accent colour wherever it is the most flattering.

If your legs aren't as shapely as you'd like them to be, or your feet are bigger than you like them to be, don't wear an accent colour in your shoes, particularly in bright tones and most particularly in white. White is a brilliant colour, and enlarging. Dazzling white is okay on a tennis court, but white needs to connect with a predominantly white outfit or white pants. With other AM colours, pure white can look crisp and clean in the summer, or in the tropics, but, as I have pointed out, white is not a neutral and cannot go with everything. So ignore that old 'It's summer and I must have white shoes to go with everything' routine. If you're not using AM colours, you don't need white at all. Taupe is really smarter for all colourtime palettes — even when worn with white. You especially don't want white shoes to blink on and off under a darker outfit.

One particular three-colour combination is called 'triadic.' This plan uses three equidistant colours on the standard colour wheel. A conventional triadic scheme of navy, true red, and a silver of yellow might appear on the comfortable chair in Dad's den. These are all crossover colours that have wide appeal for all colourtimes, especially for men.

The same scheme could be adapted for a child's room in a crayola combination of AM bright blue, cherry red, and cheerful daybreak yellow. A Midday scheme in this trad might be china blue, dusty rose, and banana. A triadic PM possibily would be dusk blue, bordeaux, and harvest gold.

Polychromatics

When a combination includes more than three colours, it is referred to as polychromatic. The combining of more than three solid hues can seem very 'spotty' and the eye is often distracted. Yet groups of colours can be combined effectively both in clothing and in interiors. Prints, checks, and tweeds often successfully mix many more than three colours.

Polychromatic schemes are most harmonious when one hue, such as the background colour, is predominant. For example, a lounge chair of multifloral printed linen in the desert PM shades of terra cotta (background), cream, apricot, and antique turquoise, with a touch of harvest gold, might be used against terra cotta walls. Cream suedecloth chairs as accessories and a carpet of antique turquoise would complete the scheme. Terra cotta becomes the predominant colour because it occupies the largest area.

You might feel more comfortable using the harvest gold as the carpet colour and it would probably be the most popular colour choice for this particular combination. Gold is extremely versatile, blends well with many colours, and gives a feeling of warmth to a room. But the antique turquoise would provide greater contrast and be more distinctive. Either is 'correct.' They are both in the same PM colourtime. It's simply a matter of personal choice.

In clothing, a typical polychromatic combination for either men or women would be donegal wool tweed with a crossover medium grey background interspersed with tiny random flecks of navy, wine, and evergreen. Any of these colours would work in a blouse or shirt. For men in a conservative business setting, however, a lighter grey shirt with a navy or wine tie would be most appropriate.

Neutral Territory

Neutral colours can make very effective monochromatic combinations, but they can also be tricky. It's usually not too difficult to find tan pants, a camel corduroy jacket, and a beige shirt with the same undertones. But finding appliances and tile in matching or blending undertones is a real challenge. It is, however, well worth the effort. Your colourtime samples can help you avoid expensive mistakes in undertone.

Have you ever bought a shirt in bone to go with slacks of the same colour only to get home and find that they don't go together at all? Or found beige grasscloth as the perfect background for your beige lounge and then discover

The Crossovers: Nature's Most Versatile Colours

In nature's 'grand design' these colours appear everywhere. They go with all of the colourtime palettes.

Sunlight Yellow
Who doesn't love a bright, sunny day? This is the fun-loving tint that always adds a touch of warmth and cheer.

Taupe
(Greige) A combination of grey and beige, this is the perfect neutral. It's also known as mushroom, fawn, and otter because these shades blend so naturally into a wooded environment.

True Red
The balanced, bright floral color adds pizazz wherever it appears. Whether in a landscape, in a room, or on you, it's an energetic accent.

Sky Blue
Against the beautiful back drop of blue sky, our eyes and minds are accustomed to seeing nature's myriad of colors—from red tulips and lavender hyacinths to yellow jonquils.

Navy
Dark navy blue is seen in the depth of a deep body of water. Every sailor looks good in a navy blue uniform and the world knows that everything goes with the blue of blue jeans.

Terre Brun
This elegant French phrase means "dirt brown." But the tones of soil and wood make wonderful neutral and basic shades. Every shoot that emerges from the earth is poignant against brown.

Evergreen

Stately evergreen is one of Mother Nature's most faithful shades. Wherever she arranges her flowers, she never forgets green. Have you ever denied a home to a lush plant because its green leaves didn't go with your color scheme? Of course not.

Sand

Look for the lightest beige-grey taupes in the sandstone of buildings, the wet sand and pebbles of beaches. Once you discover the terrific taupes, especially as an accessory color, you'll always want them in your closet.

Robert Hickey

Deep Wine

The deepest and most elegant of the reds, this color is as delicious as the vine-ripened fruit which inspired it. Every year is a good year for this timeless vintage shade.

Photo courtesy W. Atlee Burpee and Company

Pearl Grey

The lightest, most neutral grey of a snowy sky is also seen in the very first light of dawn. It's an undertone to the blue sky, and adds subtle depth to the blue-grey dusk.

Raisin

A brother to brown and a first cousin to wine and aubergine, raisin is the slightly purpled brown with an undertone that reminds us of the fruit from which it came.

Grey Flannel

The deeper, conservative classic is as solid as granite. Its understated elegance is an excellent foil for bright and light contrast.

Robert Hickey

Aubergine

In French it means eggplant, in clothing and interiors it means a classic deep purpled maroon. It blends tastefully into many color schemes.

Black

It's a perfect background for vivid contrast in clothing or interiors. Charcoal grey is so close to black, it can be used in the same dramatic or dignified ways.

Photo courtesy W. Atlee Burpee and Company

Herb Eiseman

Plate J

that the colours don't even come close? Although it is not necessary to find colours that match perfectly (it's better to look for a blend than a match because dye lots are never exactly the same), undertones should always blend. Straw baskets, wicker, hemp, and macrame are useful natural elements that can blend into almost any background.

> Grey is another great neutral that lends itself well to monochromatic combinations. There are warm PM greys and cool AM greys, but the most versatile greys of all are the balanced, crossover Pearl and Grey Flannel, and charcoal. These are the greys that blend with every colour-time. (See examples in Crossover Colours.)

Terrific Taupe

Taupe is the neutral that gets the gold star for versatility. It is the happy union of beige and grey, with several different undertones. A pinkish mauve undertone works with most AM colours. A golden (and sometimes greenish) undertone works with most PM colours. The best taupe for the Midday palette is a medium grey-beige, often named 'mushroom,' with neutral, barely discernible undertones.

Because of their versatility and the fact that they are actually a blend of two neutrals, all taupes are crossover colours. I suggest the warm taupe for blending with the warm colours in all colourtimes, and the cool mauve taupe for blending with the cool colours in all colourtimes. The crossover middle-value taupe known as greige blends with all colourtimes. It is also called 'otter,' and 'fawn.' The lighter crossover taupe called 'sand' is also a terrific neutral taupe. Once you discover taupe (if you haven't yet), you'll wonder how you ever managed without it.

People who like the Midday palette best have a strong affinity for neutral colours, especially in interiors, perhaps because they recognize how well neutrals complement the muted ice-cream tints of Midday.

Neutral colours are excellent budget stretchers because they blend well, are basic and dependable, are not trendy, never offensive, and make excellent background colours. They are also marvelous foils for bright accents. It is much easier on the bank account to use temporarily tempting colours in accents like silk flowers, pillows, and lampshades. Such accessories cost relatively little and can be changed much more easily than large pieces.

Accent colours may come and go according to what is 'in,' but a neutral background conveys a feeling of permanence and style.

Instant Irritants and Dramatic Discord

For colour at its most harmonious, avoid using opposite colourtime palettes of AM and PM *in equal amounts* in the brightest intensities. They will fight for attention on your body, and in a room they will look overdone, busy, and just plain uncomfortable or irritating. Combining the sparkling jewel tones of the AM with the fiery tones of the PM can be tiresome and even tacky.

If the kids spend too much time in the bathroom, try equal amounts of a strong AM fuchsia and a PM burnt orange in a big floral print, and they'll get out in a hurry. The only problem is that you won't want to stay in there either. A client's husband threatened to paint the spare bedroom in a thoroughly obnoxious combination of colours if any more relatives came to visit. He told me that he gave up on the idea when he realized that his in-laws would probably love it!

Discord can be very dramatic if used in the right proportions. Various tones of earthy bronze and warm PM beiges could have a smidgin of sapphire blue thrown in to gain attention, and a dash of cool regal purple against a PM cinnamon is certainly different and dramatic. Discord isn't always ugly if you follow the guidelines of dominance and subordination. But it's not for the fainthearted or basically practical person.

It takes a talented designer with a real flair for colour to use odd or highly unusual combinations, but you can create unusual combinations within your colourtime and not run the risk of looking eccentric.

What if somebody gives you a gift that is a discordant combination of colours? You may not particularly like it, but if your brand new mother-in-law gives it to you, you feel you have to show up in it. Let's assume that it's a bulky (and itchy) wool V-necked cardigan in her (not your) favourite shades of horizon purple. You are a Midday and really are not turned on at all to those particular purples. They make your complexion kind of grey (nauseous green might come closer). What can you do?

If you wear a checked cotton shirt with the collar out of the V-neck, it will not only solve the itchies, it will also do what I call 'breaking the colour line.' Allowing other colours next to your face to reflect in your hair, skin, and eyes keeps the purple from being right up under your chin. The shirt might have a single line of purple running through the pattern; the other colours could be softened Midday colours such as mauve, vanilla, and lilac.

The small amount of purple in the shirt would blend with the cardigan — remember that it doesn't have to match perfectly. The other colours will be all in your colourtime so you have a happy solution.

Phyllis Diller has made fantastic use of discord in what she calls her 'wild colours.' She says she loves 'sparkling, unheard-of combinations'... and that shocking pink is her best performing colour. True red is wonderful and 'up,' but wine is a bit 'down.' Forget purple and black for Phyllis – they depress her.

She really does have an excellent colour sense and interestingly enough, in her off-stage hours, prefers the light colours, especially monochromatic beiges and grey in clothing.

Bette Midler assembles some of the zaniest discordant combinations for the stage – all done with a wonderfully tacky flair. But in her civilian hours, she retreats into the more subdued combinations of her PM palette.

Many people, when they choose clothes, are confused about what goes with what in accessories because trends change so rapidly. In order to make your choices easier, I've listed the following guidelines:

Accessorising With Colour

Shoes

A good 'when in doubt' guideline is to keep shoe colours the same tone as your hemline, or make them a deeper shade. At one time in fashion, it was the only way to go. Now there are some exceptions to this rule:

1. When you wear pants, shoes are not as outstanding as they are with a skirt or a dress because an elongated line is created through the leg. But let your eye be the judge. If shoes are too bright, light, white, or shiny, they may be distracting and bring the eye to the feet first (you don't want your feet to be a focal point, especially if you're self-conscious about your shoe size).

2. When wearing over-the-calf (not short) boots, the leg appears elongated, so it is not necessary to match the hemline. However, the figure is lengthened even more when the hemline and boot do match. For an even longer line, match stockings to boots.

3. Boots could blend, match, or relate to something in the top of the outfit. For example: A crossover shirt of true red, navy, and evergreen with jeans and red boots.

4. When wearing a light-to-medium value or neutral colour, neutral shoes work best. They may be somewhat lighter, darker, or the same tone as the hemline. For example: a PM coral dress with light camel shoes, or an AM orchid dress with grey shoes.

Taupe is definitely the most versatile of all neutrals, since it goes with almost all colours, except for very dark shades. Which brings us to our next guideline.

5. Very dark hues in an outfit *do* need dark shoe colours. Black, navy, dark purple, wine, raisin, charcoal grey, deep evergreen, aubergine, brown, etc. need to be supported by dark shoes. Neutral shoes would be too light. In fashion, this is called stability – the balancing of the darker shades on the upper body with those of the lower body. This is especially important to anyone whose proportions are wider below than they are above. The most versatile of all the dark accessory colours for shoes are the crossover shades of wine, aubergine, and raisin. They blend with more shades than black does.

6. Shoes may be dyed to match, especially when the colour is unusual. This is usually a very dramatic or fun approach, but it's not absolutely necessary. If you like to 'play' with colours, experiment on an older pair of shoes in fairly good condition. A deep emerald green long dress might be beautiful with matching shoes (if you can get them to match!), but strippy black sandals would work, too, and be far more practical.

7. Silver metallics look best with cool colours and gold works best with warm colours.

Stockings

A good rule of thumb is to blend the colour of your stockings with the colour of your shoes. It makes you look 'leggier,' and it's especially sexy in neutrals such as taupe. Models and actresses like **Lauren Bacall** often uses this look on stage.

If you're the trendy type and want to use light stockings when they're in style, use something light at the top of the body, such as a blouse, a scarf, a collar, or jewelry as a connecting link to your face and to create good balance.

Dark stockings do not always make your legs look slimmer and light stockings do not always make your legs look heavier. It depends strictly on how you put the look together. Navy stockings under a light grey skirt will draw the eye directly to the point where the two colours come together and enlarge the legs by creating a horizontal line, but light sand stockings under a sand skirt create a longer line, especially when coordinated with sand shoes.

These are the basic 'families' of stocking colours. Trends come and go, but these are the classic combinations:

1. TAUPE – This is the grey-beige 'when in doubt' shade that blends with so many clothing colours. It's at its best with taupe and shades of grey or green. It is also a good shade when you'd rather not wear anything too dark with blacks and browns.

2. BEIGE TO MEDIUM BROWN – These shades go best with bone, off-white, tans, etc. Be careful to choose the proper undertones. Generally, the AMs are cooler, PMs warmer; Midday is a combination of the two. Cool pinky AM beige stockings would be horrendous with a warm PM camel beige shoe. Your legs would look as if they had turned red. If you are in doubt about colourtime, compare several shades and you will see the undertones. Your colourtime swatches may also help.

3. GREY TO OFF-BLACK – Best with grey and black, also possible with navy. Avoid beige with grey or black.

4. NEUTRAL – The best way to describe a neutral stocking is to say that it matches your skin shade. This is the stocking to wear when you want your leg colour to be as unobtrusive as possible. For example: A slinky red dress with matching shoes makes enough of a statement without red stockings, too. Neutral hose would also be worn with white shoes.

5. WINE, AUBERGINE, and RAISIN – Outfits in these crossover colours need stockings that blend.

6. VERY DARK AND VERY LIGHT – Trend colours, such as pastels, dark or bright opaques will change according to the latest fashion. The general guideline is to blend to your shoe colour, but for a fun look, blend to a colour in the top of your outfit.

Handbags

Remember when handbags had to match shoes? Now the key word is 'mood.' As long as they are both sporty or dressy, forget all the old rules. The bag may still match your shoes, but it could also be lighter or somewhat darker, as long as the undertone is similar.

The neutral colour is the most favoured, practical way to go, most especially in taupe. Your bag may also match something in the body of the outfit, such as a belt, or it may be in a pattern that blends with your shoes or outfit.

Belts

Belts can be an interesting colour accent. They may match your shoes, your bag, or a colour in the body of your outfit, or they may blend with other accessories like jewellery or scarves. A belt will draw attention to the waist if its colour contrasts with the background. That same colour should be repeated in one or two additional spots on the body. Remember, a solid accent colour should be used in no more than three places on the body or the look becomes spotty and distracting.

Jewellery

Since there are warm and cool colours in all palettes, silver and gold have a place in each colourtime. The type of finish determines where it looks best. Shiny silvers and platiniums work well with the cool AM jewel tones, and shiny gold with the warm AM tones. There are more warm colours in the PM, so Florentine golds and deep coppers complement the warm tones; and pewters, brushed, and antique silver look best with cool PM colours. Middays may use either, but favour the delustered finishes.

Gold is the equivalent of sunlight yellow and blends with all palettes. Silver and gold can be worn together, but it is best to keep the finishes compatible, such as brassy gold with shiny silver or brushed gold with antiqued silver.

White, bright fresh water pearls look best against AM colours or complexions. Creamy natural pearls work best against PM colours or complexions. Again, Midday people may choose either, depending on the undertones of the colours they are wearing.

Precious stones and gems are so highly reflective that they often blend with or pick up surrounding shadings. Iridescent stones such as opals seem to change according to available light, just as fabrics with a sheen do.

Some stones are so definite in their deep, bright, greyed, or honeyed intensity that they look best with other definite AM, Midday, or PM colours. For example, a dazzlingly bright aquamarine with a matching or blending AM tone, or melony coral with soft Midday values. Amber and topaz are usually PM preferences. Let your eye be your guide. At one time greys were only worn with silver. Now we see gold against charcoal and it looks marvellous. Except for a rare or unusual stone, or a very flawed stone, diamonds are so highly reflective that they work with everything – the perfect 'crossover' jewel!

Cosmetics and Colours

The Colour Clock can save you money by helping you choose the right cosmetic shade every time you buy. As every woman knows, it is easy to accumulate a drawerful of rejects – the makeup base that turned out to be the wrong shade and made you look like you were wearing a mask, or the lipstick that looked terrific on your best friend but just didn't make it on you.

Expensive mistakes like this can add up – a lot of money can go down the tube along with the lipsticks. I always recommend trying before buying. Certain shades look totally different on the skin than they do in the container. And sometimes a reaction to body chemistry (oilness, ruddy tones, sallowness, etc.) will change a shade after it has been on the skin for a while.

Always try to buy cosmetics after you've been able to keep them on for a time. Ideally, the products should be applied first, as they are in a demonstration. This is the best way to go – you're unhurried, relaxed, and have a chance to see what the finished product looks like. Try to check yourself in daylight. If it isn't possible, then be sure to use good lighting.

There is nothing mysterious about choosing the correct cosmetic colours. The guidelines that follow can take the guesswork out of it. If you're like most of my clients, you buy too many colours and invariably go back to using your old reliable favorites. Chances are, these favourites are in your personal colourtime and that's why you like them. But to help you avoid expensive mistakes (there are no more inexpensive mistakes), remember these pointers when you choose your most basic cosmetics:

1. Every colourtime palette has both warm and cool colours, even though the AM tones are predominantly cool, PM tones predominantly warm, and Midday a balance of both. You simply need two 'sets' of basics – lipstick, blush, and nail polish – one in the warm range of your colourtime, and the other in its cool tones. If you're in the AM colourtime and use many of the cool colours, you will still need a warmer tone to wear with the daffodil and daybreak yellows, rose-pink corals, and cocoa browns. PM people will use up their warm colours first, but need a cool tone to wear with blues, greens, and purples. Middays are likely to make equal use of their warm and cool tones.

Use your colourtime palette as a guide in choosing your shades. Don't try to match your palette perfectly; simply look for a blend. If your lipstick turns blue no matter what you wear (many people have that problem), try a yellow lipstick under it. If your lips go orange, try a flesh tone as an undercoat.

2. One basic makeup base should blend with your skin tone. Match it as closely as possible so that it doesn't look masklike. You will have to do a lot of experimenting, but it's worth it to get the right shade. Use a colourless, translucent powder over any makeup shade so that the base colour doesn't change.

3. Eye shadow colours can vary – your choices include:
a. The colour of the undertones in your eyes, such as teal shadow with blue-green eyes, or amber with brown eyes.
b. A complementary colour that intensifies the colour of your eyes, such as taupe for blue eyes, or a dusty rose for green eyes. The colour wheel illustration can help you to choose complementary shades, which are suggested by many cosmetic companies. The brightest shade of your 'opposite' eye colours on the

colour wheel would be too intense, so you would need to darken or lighten it.
c. You might want to match your eye shadow colour to your outfit. A very special colour, say a dusty lilac, can be dramatically accentuated with a blending eye shadow.

Let your colourtime colours guide your choice of eye shadow colours. Keep your shadow subtle. Dust it down with some taupe or grey so that it shadows, not overshadows your eyes. Basic mascara colours are black for dark lashes, dark brown for light lashes. Navy is good for blue-eyed people.

The following chart contains some colour names to help you make your choices. Shades, of course, vary with the manufacturer. These are simply descriptive terms to help you differentiate between the three colourtime palettes. If you have the kind of skin tone that defies every rule, you might have to experiment more than most.

Sunrise (AM)

Most bases in your colourtime will have a very fair or slightly rose-pink or rose-brown undertone. If the base becomes too pink on the skin, go to a straight beige or brown with no discernible undertone and add your colour by using blusher on your cheeks, chin, and forehead (just a touch). This is far better than using a shade that is so different from your skin tone that it creates a mask-like line of demarcation.

AM make-up base shades have names like:

Rose Beige	Rose-Brown
Cool Beige	Cocoa
Light Beige	Fair

Blushers, rouges, lipsticks, glosses, and nail polishes will often have a blue-pink, rose-brown or rose-wine cast. The name will often tell you where to classify the colour in the clock. Typical names include:

Ruby Red	Iced Mauve
Wine and Roses	Porcelain Rose
Sea Shell	Cherry Brown
Glazed Pink	Frosted Lavender
Rose Coral	

Adjectives used to describe gems are often a clue to AM shades. They are called: 'icy,' 'glistening,' 'gleaming,' 'glossy,' 'glazed,' 'crystal,' 'diamond,' 'sparkling,' 'frosted,' 'super-frosted,' 'silvered,' or 'brightest.'

Sunset (PM)

PM complexions will have a warm undertone. If there is any pink in the skin, it is warm and peachy – not the rosy pink of AM. Honey, cream, and golden are often used as adjectives to describe PM make-up base shades, which have names like:

Warm Beige	Rachel
Creamy Beige	Deep Tan
Honey Beige	Coffee Bronze
Peach	Amber

PM blushers, rouges, lipsticks, glosses, and nail polishes have tones of warm pink (such as coral), browned burgundy, golden brown and other tawny tones. These Sunset colours are often called:

Brandied Apricot	Burnished Plum
Copper	Golden Coral
Sienna	Indian Earth
Burnt Almond	Bordeaux Wine
Ginger Peachy	

Descriptive terms for PM shades include 'mellow,' 'dusky,' 'honeyed,' 'golden,' 'tawny,' 'brandied,' 'amber,' 'burnt,' 'shadowed,' 'slate,' 'coppery,' or 'heather.' They may have a sheen, as in 'copper frost,' but they are generally 'earthier' than AM shades.

Sunlight (Midday)

Sunlight complexions are characterized by a combination of undertones. If you're in this colourtime your best makeup shade is usually a balanced beige with equal amounts of warm and cool undertones. These shades are often called:

Natural Beige	Ivory
Medium Beige	Bisque
Soft Beige	Mocha (for slightly darker skin)
Basic Beige	Natural Tan (for slightly darker skin)

When in doubt, try a natural beige tone that blends with your skin and add blusher to cheeks, chin, and forehead.

Sunrise (A.M.) Fool-Proof Combinations

The twenty-four combinations illustrated below are among the best 'fool-proof' possibilities in the Sunrise palette. Some are classic and conservative, appropriate for a business suit, like monochromatic Grey Flannel and Crystal Grey. Others are more creative and fun, better for a bathing suit, like Sunlight Yellow and Limeade. Choose whatever combinations suit your needs, but use these suggestions to open yourself up to new possibilities. For example, one of the best ways to recycle a favourite navy jacket is to wear it with an emerald blouse or a touch of emerald in your tie. It will seem new again to you and everyone who sees it.

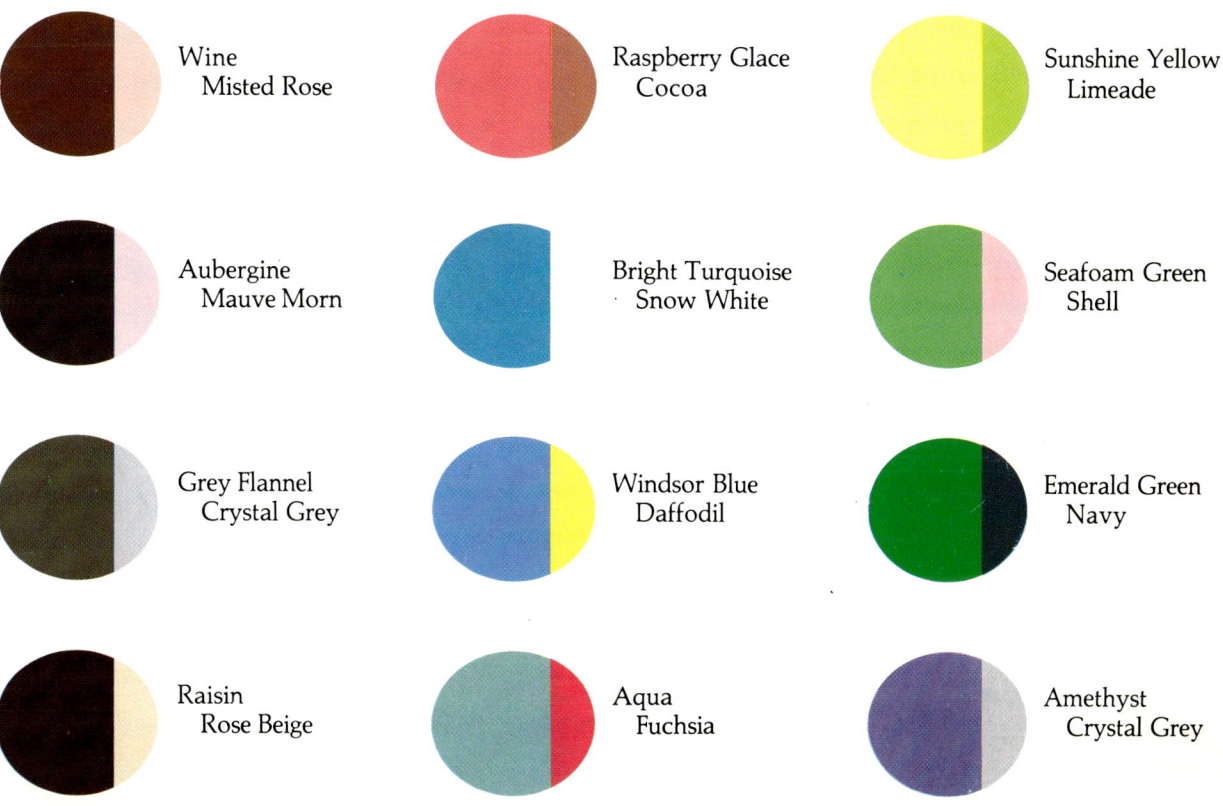

Plate K

If you want to stretch your budget, use neutrals and basic colours. Make taupe, beige, grey, or deep basic shades like aubergine, raisin, wine, brown, navy, and charcoal part of your combinations. They are all classics that will work especially well as accessories for many colours.

For successful balance, one colour is dominant, the second subordinate and the third an accent. Any colour in your palette's combinations may be the dominant, subordinate or accent colour. See Chapters 2, 3 and 4 for a complete discussion on using more than three colours together, plus additional 'how-to's' for clothing and interiors.

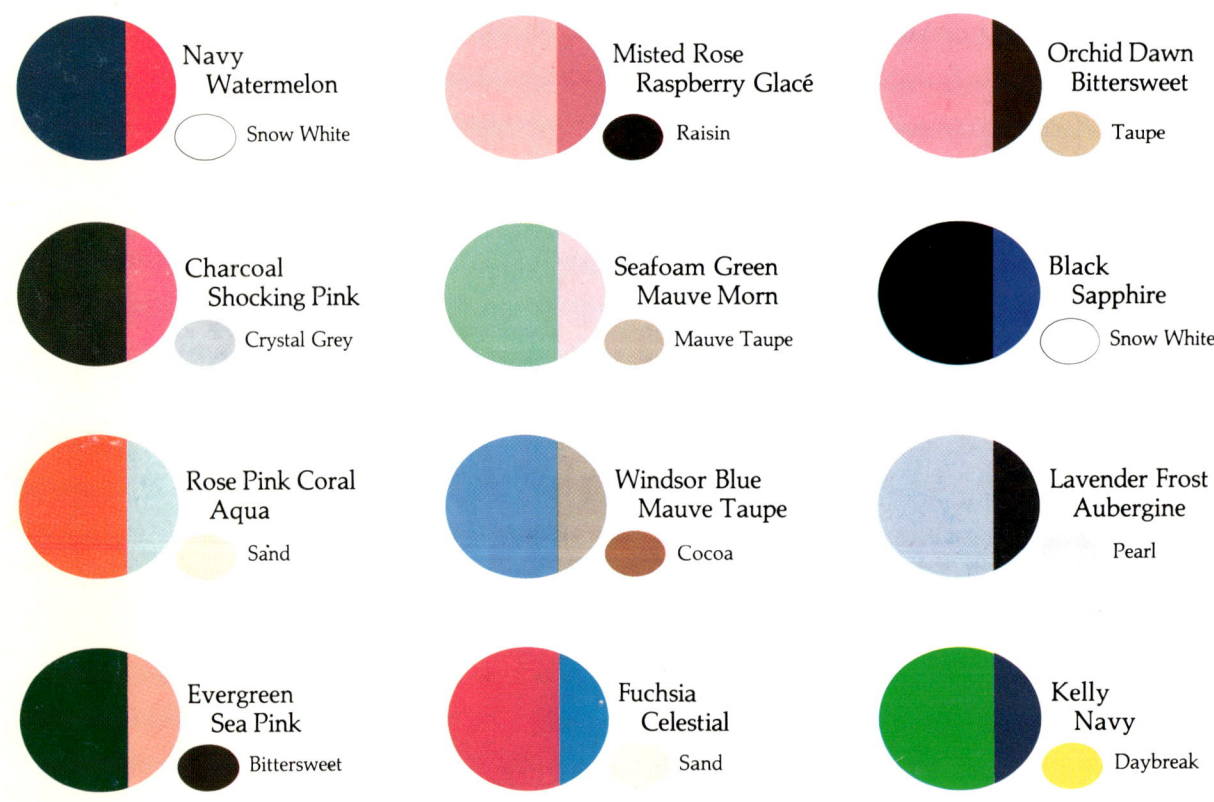

The Midday colours are subtle, muted, and delicious — fresh fruit sherbet shades. Eye shadows are in subtle neutral tones.

Sunlight blushers, rouges, lipsticks, glosses, and nail polishes have names like:

<table>
<tr><td>Blushing Peach</td><td>Rosewood</td></tr>
<tr><td>Midday Rose</td><td>Chestnut</td></tr>
<tr><td>Fresh Melon</td><td>Gentle Grape</td></tr>
</table>

Since the Midday colours dip into both of the other two palettes, you might also try the subtler shades from both the AM and PM palettes.

Crossover colours in makeup shades may be used by all palettes; such shades as aubergine, raisin, deep wine, and true red often make beautiful basics, If you are wearing red, but don't like red lips, deepen the colour with a bit of brown or outline your lips in red and fill in with a softer shade.

Can You Change Your Colourtime Cosmetics?

Is it possible to switch from one colourtime to another by changing makeup base shades? Yes, but tricky. Since you don't want that line of demarcation where the makeup base ends, it is best to closely match your skin. But if you do want to switch occasionally, blend very carefully at the jawline by using a slightly dampened sea sponge to carry the colour down on the neck.

You can change your lipstick and blusher to blend with the base. The really tricky part is changing your natural eye colour! Coloured contact lenses are one solution (but it's quite expensive). If you have hazel eyes, it's less difficult because these are the chameleon shades that tend to reflect the colour you wear nearest your face.

Another obstacle to changing colourtimes is hair colour. You certainly wouldn't want to change your hair colour every other day. Wigs are passé. Scarves and hats are in, but because you don't wear your hat with your nightgown, you eventually have to face the moment of truth.

So you can fool Mother Nature; it's not impossible, but it is difficult. If you keep switching colourtimes, however, you'll have to have all the right shades in that particular palette.

Models and actresses must make frequent colour changes, but wide-ranging makeup shades are part of the tools of their trade. **Jeff Angell** is an award winning Hollywood makeup artist who works with many of the top models and stars in films and TV. What he does to a face is pure magic! He often changes a model's colourtime for cosmetic ads, but the lighting is also changed. Since we can't all walk around (unfortunately) with special lights focused on us at all times, it is most flattering to stay in your own colourtime, especially for daytime makeup.

Jeff feels that most women don't experiment enough with makeup. He suggests applying samples of your makeup base, eye colours, lipsticks, and blushers on cardboard (not white paper) to see how a particular group of colours is going to look together. It's a trick that he uses that can help you decide if you like the way they blend and alert you to possible mistakes. He also feels, and I agree with him, that white makeup under the eyes can accentuate circles rather than hide them. Try an off-white or flesh tone instead.

Most women prefer a few dependable eyeshadow colours, a basic makeup and blusher shade, and a few lip colours. Once you have the basics, you can have fun with the extras. And it really is fun to play with new colours. Nothing dates a woman more than an antiquated hairstyle or an outmoded lipstick shade. Fuschia may have been fascinating on her when she was twenty, but time does march on. It is impossible to have a single lipstick shade that 'goes with everything.'

You may have trouble with 'odd' shades that are difficult to find the right lipstick for. Rather than try to match a blue-wine sweater with a lot of brown undertone, for example, buy a shade like Wine and Roses (AM) and blend it with Burnished Brown (PM). Or get out some of your rejects (the ones you can't bring yourself to throw away) and try them with a new colour. See how inventive and creative you can be. A word of caution – be careful of intensely purpled or very blue-based lipsticks if your teeth are yellowed. Soften the blue undertone or warm it up slightly.

Hair Colour

If you colour your hair, choosing the right shade can be more confusing than choosing cosmetics. The name of the colour will generally give you a good idea of whether it is AM, Midday, or PM – Arctic Blonde (AM), Honey Blonde (PM), and Neutral Blonde (Midday), for example. The photo on the box or in an illustrated brochure can be a fairly good indicator of the colour inside. Many terms are either not descriptive enough or too difficult to classify by name. 'Frivolous Fawn' or 'Bashful Beige' might be anybody's guess!

Body chemistry can affect hair just as it does cosmetics. Your hair may have a natural red or gold tone that has a tendency to come through whatever colour you use. You may find this an attractive undertone, especially if you have PM colouring. But if you want to play down the red-gold, use a product with either cool or ash undertones.

Conversely, if you have used a product that has given your hair a green or blue-green tinge, a reddish shade can help to neutralize the blue-green. If you are blonde or grey and have used a product that added unwanted violet or silver, a golden shade is a good neutralizer. Strange things can happen to your skin tone if your hair colouring clashes with your colourtime. Hair is a crucial part of your self-image, and it's well worth the time it takes to get the colour right.

If this seems totally confusing, not to worry. Your hairdresser can help. If you've really made a mess, let a professional undo the damage. Limit your experiments with new colours to small strands of hair until you are sure of how the colour will respond to you.

The following guidelines can help you with hair colour choices; the Colour Clock can be a tremendous help. Your natural colour is never wrong. But if you want to change it, cover it up, or enhance it, use the shades that will appear most natural.

Blondes

Sunrise
If you are an AM blonde, ash or platinium tones will blend best with your skin. A bit of yellow is all right, but brassy gold will not blend with your cool skin. You will want to eliminate as much gold as possible. The shades that most closely describe Sunrise blondes are:

Ash Blonde	Platinum
Nordic	Cool Beige

Sunset
If you are in the sun a good deal, your hair tends to turn a yellow-gold. As a PM blonde, this can be a blessing because golden undertones will blend with your skin and hair, looking terrific and natural. In choosing hair colours, PM blondes look for key words like:

Warm Blonde	Warm Beige
Golden Blonde	Amber
Honey Blonde	

Sunlight
If you are a Midday blonde, a combination of blonde shades can be very effective. Because you tend to have variety in your natural colour and your skin has both warm and cool undertones, variegated hair can be extremely flattering. Streaking or weaving is especially good on Middays; shades from the AM and PM palette may be combined.

Redheads

The term redhead covers a wide range of colours. True auburn tends to flatter AM skins because it has a relatively cool cast compared with the rust-copper undertones of a golden PM red. PM redheads with sallow or yellowed skin should be wary of intensifying golden tones, which may emphasize the sallowness; a mixture of auburn and coppery shades might work better than straight copper for these skin colours.

Red hair may have a tendency to become 'brassy.' Regardless of your colourtime, be careful of harsh tones if your skin is aging or sallow. You may have to switch to a less vivid colour to keep the brassiness out.

Sunrise
AM red shades have names like:

>   Sherry   Medium Auburn
>   Berry   Dark Auburn
>   Light Auburn

Sunset
PM red shades are apt to be called:

>   Coppertone   Red Penny
>   Sun Bronze   Honey Red
>   Reddish Blonde   Burnished Copper

Sunlight (Midday)
Midday redheads are never bright. If you're a redheaded Midday, your colour is more subtle and often streaked. Combined auburn and copper tones are a good choice. In many instances, natural redheads will go from AM or PM to Midday when their hair begins to streak with grey. The softer shades are more flattering in later years than the bright or deep tones of youth.

Redheads in every colourtime must be careful of fiery reds and oranges in clothing because they may compete or clash with their hair and overshadow it. If you're a PM redhead who loves these colours, use them as accents or in prints. Tawny shades like terra cotta, peach, warm browns, bordeaux, terre brown, apricot and raisin are better to use near your hair than brilliant orange-reds. AM auburns, with their cool red tones, look wonderful in shades of raisin, rose-pink coral, cocoa, bittersweet, and terre brun. Midday reds are terrific in melon, orange blossom, mocha, chestnut, raisin, and terre brun.

Browns

Sunrise
AM Browns usually have ash undertones, which may range from quite light to very dark. If a red tone is present, it is auburn or berry coloured.

Sunrise brown shades are often described as:

> Light Ash Brown   Dark Ash Brown
> Medium Ash Brown   Sable

Sunset
PM browns tend to accent the amber tones. Colours in this range (from lightest to darkest undertones) are often called:

> Warm Brown   Honeyed Brown
> Golden Brown   Russet

Sunlight
Midday browns are variegated combinations of warm and cool tones. The most natural looking combination will combine both the AM and PM colour-time shades.

Grey

Once upon a time, all little grey-haired ladies put blue rinses on their hair. Golden tones in grey were a definite no-no. In spite of the trend to more natural greying, most grey hair colouring products continue to boast that they will 'get the yellow out' as though it were some sort of dreaded affliction!

If you are PM, let the yellow stay *in*. Nature intended for your hair to blend with your skin and eyes. If your skin is sallow, you may want to liven up the grey somewhat by giving it sheen, which can be done with a good conditioner, or you may want to go to a warm grey rinse. These are more difficult to find than the cool AM shades and their names are often misleading. Some 'Snow Whites' and 'Pearly Whites' are in the warm range. You will simply have to experiment.

Middays look great with salt and pepper or mixed greys. But no blue tints, please, for Midday or PM. You will look absolutely ill.

A hint of blue in the silvery tones of an AM grey can be striking, but an AM risks looking dated when too much blue is added. Try a good conditioner on your natural colour. If this doesn't do it, there are lots of good AM greys on the market, with names like 'Silver,' 'Cool White,' and 'Silver Diamond.' Grey and white hair, like blonde, tends to yellow in sunlight. If you are an AM grey, remember to protect your hair from bright sunlight.

The term 'Salt and Pepper' describes those who are changing from their natural darker colour to grey. The emerging grey of AM people will show a silvery or pure white tone. A pewter grey mixture is characteristic of PMs and the greying hair of Middays tends to have both warm and cool tones.

Blacks

True blue-black is always AM. This is why tinted blue-black hair can look so phony on some people. They are Midday or PM and it simply does not go with their skin and eyes. This can make tinted black hair painfully obvious – more so than any other colour. This is especially true for men, because they lack the cosmetics to help their skin tones blend with the tinted shade.

It is also very difficult to retain blue-black hair in later years because it can be so harsh next to yellowing or aging skin. I always suggest a dark cool brown or a brown mixed with a smidgin of black for 'maturing' AMs, a mixture of medium to dark browns for Middays, and a dark honeyed brown for PMs.

Blue-black really does look best on flawless, fair, or youthful AM skin. The natural hair colour of 'black'-haired PMs, as dark as it may seem, is really deep brown or umber brown-black rather than blue-black. There is no black in the Sunlight palette.

If your hairstylist does your colouring, please introduce him or her to the Colour Clock. Hairstylists can do a fantastic job on colour without it, if they have a good eye for colour. But because not all hairstylists are colourists, they may be tempted to choose a colour simply because it is in their colourtime – not yours!

Fool-Proof Combinations

I often suggest that clients who are interested in simplifying their wardrobes start with a two-colour (duochromatic) plan. Choose both your main colour and the blending second colour from the same colourtime palette. The most practical choice, and the best way to stretch your budget, is to make that second colour a neutral or basic shade. It will also make a good accessory colour that works well with many other things in your wardrobe.

Some of the best neutrals are the crossover taupes of greige and sand, and pearl grey and grey flannel; but each colourtime palette contains other useful shades of beige, tan, grey, and taupe. Check your colourtime palette to see what they are.

The darker crossover shades that work well as accessory colours are aubergine, raisin, wine, navy, terre brun, charcoal, and black. These dependable basics always stay in fashion.

To make your choices easier, possible combinations are illustrated. The following pages will also help you choose 'fool-proof' combinations. For a duo-chromatic combination, simply use a colour from the first column (A) with a colour from either of the adjacent columns (B). For example: Midday grape and greige.

For a three colour (trichromatic) combination, the most practical choice would be one colour from 'A,' another colour from 'B,' and a third shade from one of the neutral colours listed. For example: PM Coral Dust, Brick Red, and Camel.

> When you decorate a room, you may combine colours just as you would when decorating your body. But because a room is much larger, you can use many more variations of the colours you choose. For example, the combination of AM Aqua and Mauve Morn could be expanded to include touches of Bright Turquoise and Amethyst for contrast and variety. The colours could also be combined in a print. The next chapter gives you more specific suggestions on how to handle colour in your home or office.

As you will discover later in the book, your personality definitely enters into your choices, so some of the combinations will feel just right to you, and others won't be as comfortable. Use this list as a guide.

Sunrise (AM) Fool-Proof Combinations

Column A	Column B		
Ice Blue	Opalescent Teal	Raspberry Glacé	Wine
Windsor Blue	Sapphire	Regal Purple	Greige
Celestial Blue	Amethyst	Fuchsia	Pearl Grey
Sky Blue	Orchid Dawn	Watermelon	Crystal Grey
	Aquamarine	Rose-Pink Coral	Grey Flannel
	Shocking Pink	Sea Pink	Sand
	Raisin	Aubergine	Charcoal
	Bittersweet	Mauve-Taupe	Rose-Beige
			Cocoa

Column A	Column B		
Aqua Aquamarine	Sapphire Misted Rose Raspberry Glacé Sunlight Yellow Mauve Morn Bright Turquoise Terre Brun	Orchid Dawn Sea Pink Rose-Pink Coral Daffodil Opalescent Teal Cocoa Greige	Sand Bittersweet Pearl Grey Crystal Grey Charcoal Navy
Bright Turquoise Opalescent Teal	Sapphire Celestial Blue Sea Pink Sunlight Yellow Daybreak Yellow White Crystal Grey Terre Brun	Rose-Pink Coral Shocking Pink Shell Daffodil Aqua Black Pearl Grey	Bittersweet Navy Rose-Beige Aqua Aquamarine Charcoal Mauve Taupe
Regal Purple Amethyst	Windsor Blue Sky Blue Greige Bittersweet Cocoa Mauve Morn	Ice Blue Lavender Frost Raisin Terre Brun Mauve Taupe	Grey Flannel Crystal Grey Pearl Grey White Orchid Dawn
Rose-Pink Coral Watermelon	Ice Blue Sky Blue Bright Turquoise Emerald Sunlight Yellow Seafoam Green	Celestial Blue Opalescent Teal Evergreen Rose-Beige Daffodil Navy	White Grey Flannel Crystal Grey Charcoal Pearl Grey Black
Raspberry Glacé	Opalescent Teal Sky Blue White Evergreen Lavender Frost Shell Mauve Morn Pearl Grey	Ice Blue Windsor Blue Emerald Seafoam Green Sea Pink Orchid Dawn Crystal Grey	Black Raisin Navy Cocoa Sand Charcoal Grey Flannel

Column A	Column B		
Lavender Frost	Opalescent Teal	Wine	Terre Brun
	Regal Purple	Amethyst	Bittersweet
	Raisin	Aubergine	Pearl Grey
	Aqua	Raspberry Glacé	Crystal Grey
	Windsor Blue	Greige	Grey Flannel
	Mauve-Taupe	Sand	Charcoal
Evergreen	Sky Blue	Orchid Dawn	Sand
	Rose-Pink Coral	Misted Rose	Bittersweet
	Sea Pink	Shell	Terre Brun
	Daffodil	Daybreak Yellow	Rose-Beige
	Watermelon	Navy	Cocoa
	Mauve Taupe		
Sapphire	Emerald	Windsor Blue	Terre Brun
	Bright Turquoise	Opalescent Teal	Charcoal
	Bittersweet	Black	Greige
	White	Pearl Grey	Sand
	Crystal Grey	Grey Flannel	
Emerald	Misted Rose	Shell	Navy
	Raspberry Glacé	Daybreak Yellow	Rose-Beige
	Sunlight Yellow	Sky Blue	Bittersweet
	White	Black	Terre Brun
	Crystal Grey	Pearl Grey	
Seafoam Green	Opalescent Teal	Wine	Mauve Morn
	Shocking Pink	Misted Rose	Fuchsia
	Lavender Frost	Sand	Pearl Grey
	Greige	Mauve-Taupe	Crystal Grey
	Rose-beige	Cocoa	
Daffodil	Ice Blue	Celestial Blue	Terre Brun
	Kelly Green	Windsor Blue	Grey Flannel
	Rose-Pink Coral	Limeade	Crystal Grey
	Evergreen	Bittersweet	Pearl Grey
Cherry	Ice Blue	Sky Blue	Sand
True Red	Black	Navy	Pearl Grey
	White	Charcoal	Crystal Grey
	Grey Flannel	Greige	

Sunlight *(Midday) Fool-Proof Combinations*

The twenty-four combinations illustrated here are among the best 'fool-proof' possibilities in the Sunlight palette. Some are classic and conservative – appropriate for a business suit – such as monochromatic Taupe and Tan or Mushroom and Bark. Others are more unusual and fun – great for a print – like Peach Melba and Mauve. Choose whatever combinations fit your mood or the occasion, but try to use these suggested combinations to open yourself up to all the possibilities of your palette. For example, the best way to perk tired caramel 'cords' (but still so comfortable) is to wear them with a Raspberry Sherbet sweater. That's a delicious combination!

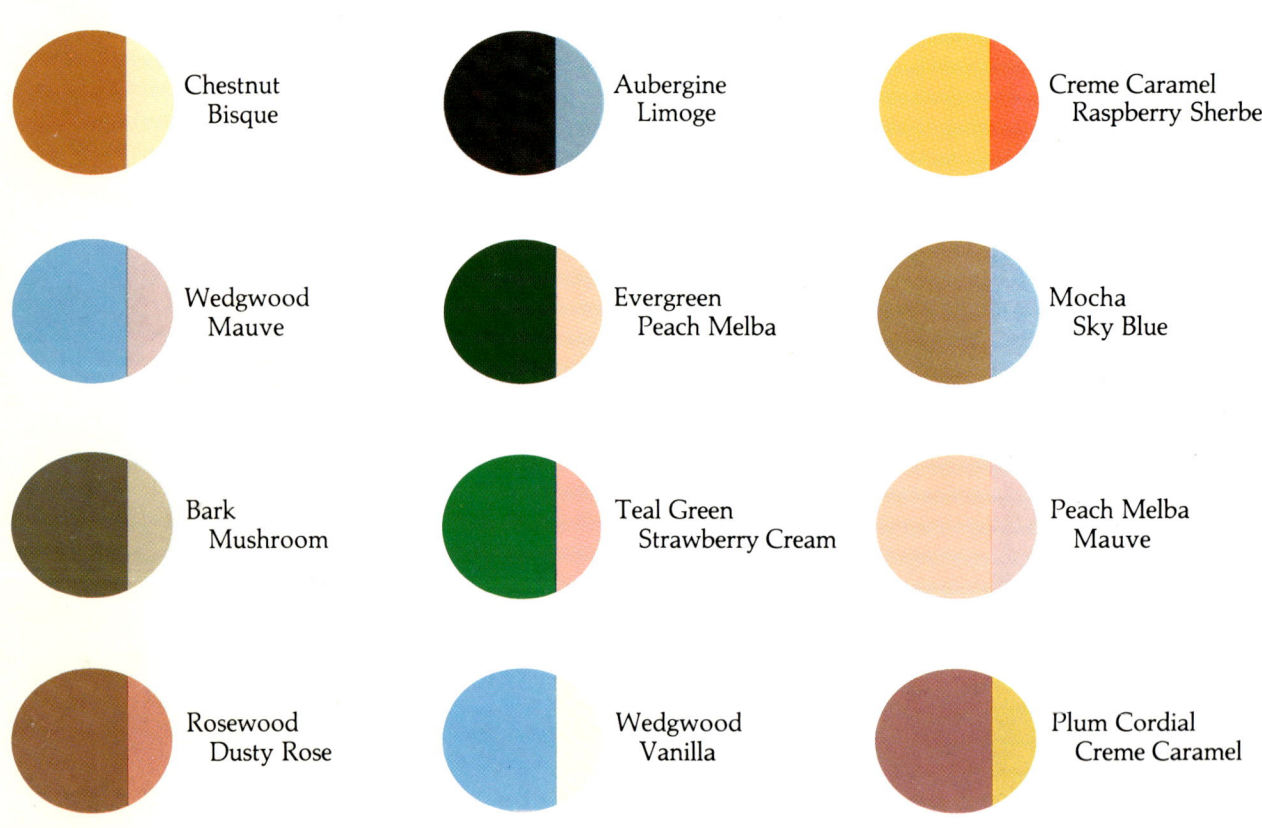

Plate M

If you want to stretch your budget, use neutrals and basics. Make taupe, tan, beige, grey, or deep basic shades like aubergine, raisin, wine, brown, navy and charcoal part of your combinations. They are all classics that work especially well as accessories.

For successful balance, one colour should be dominant, the second subordinate, and the third an accent. Any colour in your palette's combinations may be the dominant, subordinate or accent colour. See Chapters 2, 3 and 4 for a complete discussion on coordinating more than three colours, plus additional 'how-to's' on putting attractive combinations into your wardrobe and environment.

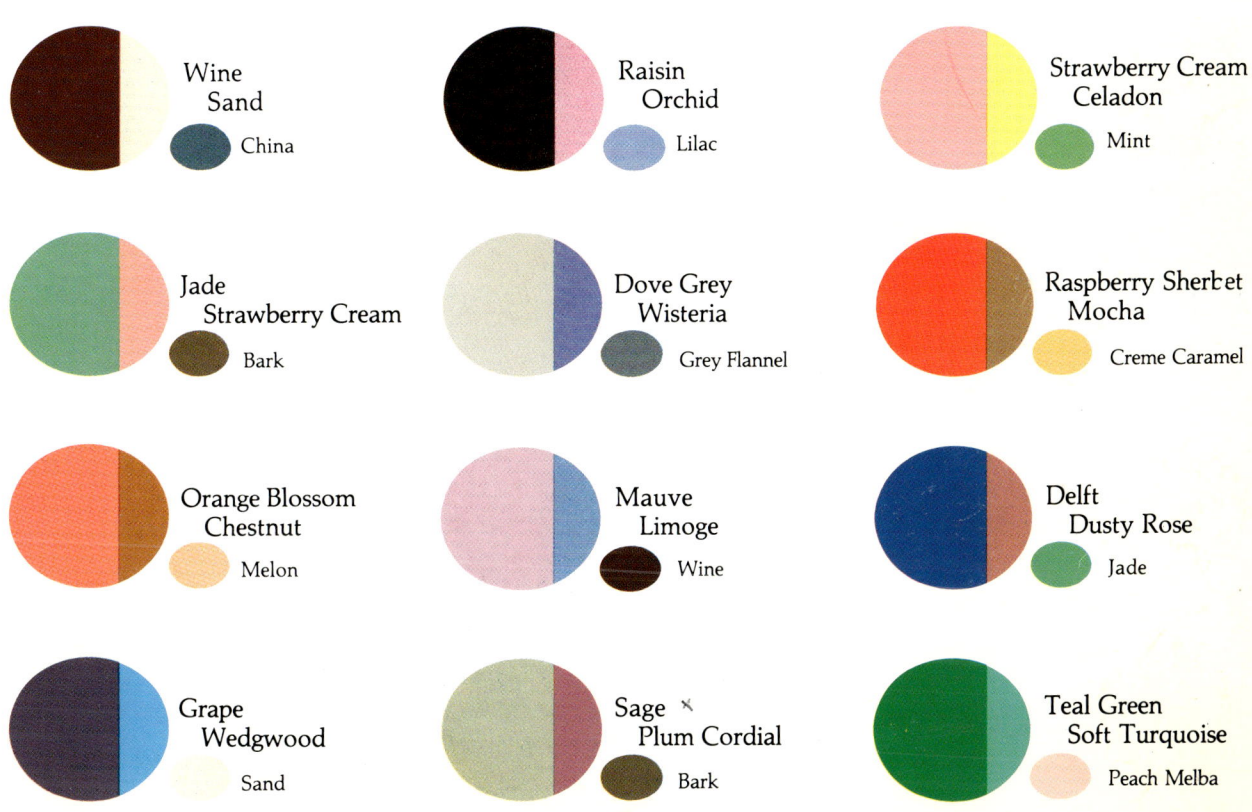

Column A	Column B			
Orchid Dawn	Sapphire	Bittersweet	Navy	
	Celestial Blue	Ice Blue	Cocoa	
	Seafoam	Black	Raisin	
	White	Mauve-Taupe	Wine	
	Greige	Pearl Grey	Aubergine	
	Crystal Grey	Fuchsia	Misted Rose	
Kelly Green	Sunlight Yellow	Daffodil	White	
Limeade	Daybreak Yellow	Shell	Charcoal	
	Terre Brun	Bittersweet	Grey Flannel	
	Sand	Mauve-Taupe	Rose-Beige	
Wine	Celestial Blue	Windsor Blue	Pearl Grey	
Aubergine	Sky Blue	Ice Blue	Greige	
Raisin	Mauve Taupe	Crystal Grey	Sand	
Ruby	Shell	Misted Rose	Aqua	
Shocking Pink	Aquamarine	White	Bittersweet	
Fuchsia	Grey Flannel	Rose-Beige	Evergreen	
	Ice Blue	Sky Blue	Black	
	Navy	Pearl Grey	Crystal Grey	

Sunset (PM) Fool-Proof Combinations

Column A	Column B			
Magenta Haze	Horizon Purple r/b	Purple Heather	Greige	
(red, white touch of blue)	Lilac Dusk r/b/w	Peacock	Smoke	
	Camel b/w	Deep Periwinkle	Pearl Grey	
	Cadet Blue b/w	Sky Blue	Grey Flannel	
	Dusk Blue b/w	Navy	Charcoal	
	Aubergine r/b/blk	Raisin	Wine	
Horizon Purple	Cadet Blue	Lilac Dusk	Sand	
Purple Heather	Greige	Cream	Brick Red	
	Magenta Haze	Raisin	Deep Periwinkle	
	Terre Brun	Dusk Blue	Smoke	
	Grey Flannel	Pearl Grey		

Column A	Column B		
Brick Red Tomato Red	Khaki Sunlight Yellow Navy Terre Brun Honey Greige Cinnamon	Autumn Gold Curry Cream Black Purple Heather Avocado	Bay Leaf Camel Warm Taupe Smoke Grey Flannel Bronze
Paprika Geranium	Terra Cotta Cream Apricot Harvest Gold Coral Dust Sky Blue Dusk Blue Hunter	~~Dusk Blue~~ Peach Peacock Horizon Purple Deep Periwinkle Cadet Blue Khaki Black ✓	Camel Charcoal Smoke Greige Navy ✓ Honey Avocado - Grey Flannel
Curry Honey	Burnt Orange Avocado · Brick Cream Dill Paprika Deep Teal	Hunter Khaki Terre Brun Sky Blue Bay Leaf Geranium Bordeaux	Deep Periwinkle ~~Hunter~~ Evergreen - Smoke Grey Flannel Black Tomato
Coral Dust	Cadet Blue Sunlight Yellow Deep Teal Hunter Deep Periwinkle Lilac Dusk Brick Red Charcoal	Sky Blue Dusk Blue Peacock Bay Leaf Evergreen · Peach Terra Cotta Smoke	Khaki Avocado · ~~Evergreen~~ Camel Cinnamon Terre Brun Antique Turquoise Grey Flannel
Aubergine Wine *bedroom* Raisin *blue* *light purple —*	Ash Rose *— deep pink* Cadet Blue - Peacock *bright blue* Greige *Taupe* Deep Periwinkle	Dusk Blue *light aster* Sky Blue - Camel *— light taupe* Warm Taupe *— L.brown* Pearl Grey *— silver*	Smoke *= donkey* Magenta Haze ✓ Lilac Dusk *— light magenta* Sand *V. L. taupe*

65

Column A	Column B		
Bordeaux	Deep Teal	Dill	Deep Periwinkle
	Khaki	Camel	Sky Blue
	Cadet Blue	Dusk Blue	Coral Dust
	Peacock	Cream	Smoke
	Greige	Warm Taupe	Pearl Grey
	Ash Rose	Lilac Dusk	
Bronze	Curry	Harvest Gold	Smoke
	Navy	Black	Honey
	Charcoal	Cream	
Deep Teal	Cinnamon	Terra Cotta	Apricot
	Cadet Blue	Dusk Blue	Peach
	Sand	Greige	Ash Rose
	Cream	Magenta Haze	~~Greige~~
	Lilac Dusk	Coral Dust	Smoke
	Navy		
True Red	Black	Charcoal	Cream
	Navy	Smoke	Camel
	Pearl Grey	Khaki	Greige
	Sand		
Antique Turquoise	Cinnamon	Terra Cotta	Honey
	Sand	Peacock	Cream
	Navy	Greige	Grey Flannel
	Warm Taupe	Curry	Charcoal
	Smoke	Black	
Hunter bottle green	Ash Rose	Coral Dust	Harvest Gold
Evergreen	Warm Taupe	Greige	Curry
Dill bright green	Honey	Apricot	Sunlight Yellow
	Peach	Paprika	Smoke
	Cinnamon	Camel	Khaki
	Cream	Brick Red	Geranium
Bay Leaf	Terra Cotta	Apricot	Sunlight Yellow
Jigsaw T.shirt	Coral Dust	Harvest Gold	Brick Red
	Warm Taupe	Greige grey/beige	Tomato
	Sand	Khaki	Burnt Orange
	Avocado	Bronze	

Column A	Column B		
Burnt Orange	Apricot	Peach	Terre Brun
	Sunlight Yellow	Harvest Gold	Bay Leaf
	Honey	Terra Cotta	Avocado
	Paprika	Navy	Khaki
	Charcoal	Smoke	Sand
	Cream	Camel	

Sunlight (Midday) Fool-Proof Combinations

Column A	Column B		
Peach Melba Melon	Evergreen	Teal Green	Mocha
	Creme De Menthe	Mint	Terre Brun
	Mauve	Vanilla	China Blue
	Mushroom	Terre Brun	Orange Blossom
	Dove	Pearl Grey	Soft Turquoise
	Grey Flannel	Jade	Lilac
	Wedgwood	Delft	Chestnut
	Limoges		
Dusty Rose Strawberry Cream	Evergreen	Plum Cordial	Mocha
	Soft Turquoise	China Blue	Sand
	Sky Blue	Teal Green	Dove
	Mauve	Jade	Pearl Grey
	Raisin	Rosewood	Creme Caramel
	Limoges	Wedgwood	Greige
	Grape	Mint	Aubergine
	Wine		
China Blue Sky Blue	Grape	Mocha	Dove
	Wine	Mauve	Pearl Grey
	Banana	Raspberry Sherbet	Grey Flannel
	Plum Cordial	Sage	Aubergine
	Mauve	Dusty Rose	Raisin
	Orchid	Sunlight Yellow	Wine
	Creme Caramel	Peach Melba	Sand
	Bisque	Terre Brun	Mushroom
	Greige		

Column A	Column B		
Raisin Aubergine Wine	Strawberry Cream Mauve Orchid Wedgwood Greige	Dusty Rose China Blue Limoges Lilac Sand	Mushroom Dove Pearl Grey Sky Blue
Chestnut Creme Caramel	Vanilla China Blue Melon Bisque Orchid Delft Black	Teal Green Peach Melba Mauve Wisteria Orange Blossom Terre Brun Pearl Grey	Dove Grey Flannel Sand Navy Grape Dusty Rose
Banana Buttercream Lemonade	Mint Creme de Menthe Orange Blossom Celadon Soft Turquoise Greige	China Blue Melon Chestnut Limoges Dove	Delft Sky Blue Navy Pearl Grey Grey Flannel
Creme de Menthe	Strawberry Cream Dusty Rose Melon Mocha Bark Lemonade	Raspberry Sherbet Banana Peach Melba Mauve Bisque	Sunlight Yellow Dove Pearl Grey Grey Flannel Greige
Jade	Teal Green Strawberry Cream Bark Bisque China Blue	Dusty Rose Melon Raspberry Sherbet Greige Pearl Grey	Sage Orchid Navy Dove Mushroom

I encourage my clients to play with their colour combinations, just as a child does with a box of crayons. You might come up with combinations that are not listed. You can open yourself up to a whole new creative experience. Don't be concerned about how someone else might do it – choose your colourtime and let your colours be an expression of you.

Keep an open mind to the excitement of new and interesting colour combinations in your chosen colourtime and see how you can come alive with colour!

Confessions of a Wardrobe Organizer

I have spent years in clients' cupboards and wardrobes. Now that's it's out in the open, I can tell you that once I get started on someone's wardrobe there is no stopping me. I'm like a scene out of one of those old Keystone Cop movies or a Benny Hill TV show where all of the characters flail their arms and run around nonstop.

There is nothing I like to do more for a client than to rearrange, weed out, sort out, and recycle. It's instant gratification for me and my client. I can also get some instant insight into a client's personality and lifestyle through the colours he or she wears. If you're like most people, opening your wardrobe door and finding it neat, efficient, and attractive makes you feel so 'together.' Somehow, when your wardrobe is organized, you feel as though your whole life is organized. (If only that were true!)

The very best time to get your wardrobe together is when you are redecorating or repainting. Everything is a mess anyhow, so a little more mess can't possibly hurt. You have to have everything out of the wardrobe anyway, unless you're one of those sneaky people who repaints a whole house but never touches the 50-year-old wallpaper in the wardrobe. I view my wardrobes and cupboards in much the same way my mother viewed clean underwear. You never know when you might be involved in an accident and get carted off to a hospital – and you just never know when someone is going to open the door to your wardrobe!

The key to a wonderfully arranged wardrobe is colour. When you are really ready to get into it, the following guidelines can give you a plan of action:

1. Pull out anything you haven't worn in a year and put it on the bed.

2. Separate day clothes from evening clothes. Put them in different sections of the wardrobe.

3. Keep all of the same kinds of clothing together. Blouses and/or shirts together, pants together, skirts together, suits, etc.

4. Arrange them by colour.

5. Throw away all your shoeboxes (unless you have x-ray vision) and put your shoes in see-through plastic containers. Writing on the outside of cardboard boxes doesn't work – you usually can't remember what the 'black casuals' look like! Keep your shoes at eye level or above if possible, so that you don't have to crawl around on all fours groping for them.

6. Organize your handbags, socks, and/or stockings, and underwear, and put them in see-through plastic containers. Especially stockings and socks – it really takes the frustration out of fishing through the black, browns, and navies when you keep them separated by colour.

7. Try to get as much as possible out of bureau drawers and onto shelves so that you can see exactly what you have. I've discovered things in bureau drawers that my clients hadn't seen in years. If you don't see it, you don't use it. Haven't you ever brought something home from the shop only to discover eventually that you had something just like it – that you had simply forgotten about it?

8. Get a piece of peg-board and assorted metal hanging hooks from your local hardware or building supply shop. If your wardrobe space is big enough, put it up on a wall or on the back of a door. If you don't have the space, use a bedroom, bathroom, or dressing room wall. This is where you're going to hang your costume jewelry and belts – all by colour on the metal hooks placed in the peg-board. This is also a good place to hang odd things that don't seem to go anyplace else.

9. Put a piece of thin foam rubber over some wire hangers and hang your scarves or ties from them. Arrange them by colour. They won't slide off and you won't have to iron the wrinkles out of your scarves every time you wear them.

The ideal wardrobe has double-hung rods so that you can keep your blouses or shirts hanging above your pants and/or skirts. Since everything should be arranged by colour, you can readily see what you have in each family of colour. It is so much easier to see what goes with what.

To get back to that pile of clothes on the bed that you never wear, check them out to see why you aren't wearing them. Chances are that you have nothing to wear them with – they're usually the 'bargains' that are not in your colourtime.

If you're not wearing them because they are just a little out of date, (wide lapel, narrow lapels) but they're classic, decide if alterations are really worth it, or move them to another place, retire them permanently. You don't have to be brutal about it. You can keep anything that has real sentimental value. But the whole point is to get organized and to give yourself more space.

As you continue to buy clothing in your preferred colourtime palette, you will see how much easier and more practical it is to combine, mix and match, and enjoy your clothes as well as your colours.

Chapter 3

Using Colour With Flair All Around You

Decorating With Colour and Flair

From earliest times, people have chosen to decorate their environments with colour. Baskets, pots, textiles, the simplest tools, even the walls of primitive dwellings were embellished with colourful designs. It's possible that the earliest cave dwellers also competed to have the nicest cave on the street! People have always been fascinated with colour and used it as part of their surroundings.

Skillful set and interior designers understand the enormous effect of colour. The initial impact that a room has on you is that your senses are flooded with colour. You will often leave that room remembering colour above all else. Your home, no matter how large or small, can be transformed into something wonderful and comfortable through the creative use of colour.

Analyze any successful room and you will notice one dominant colour or family of colours. Several shades of the same colour can pull together furniture from different periods. If you are the eclectic personality who enjoys mixing periods and styles, colour can make it all cohesive.

Most people share their environments with others. If you have a flatmate, husband, wife, or children living under your roof, have them take the Colourtime Quiz. If they're all attracted to the same colourtime, you simply decorate in those colours and everybody is happy.

But what happens if two or more people who live under one roof prefer different colourtimes for decorating? Who wins out? Sometimes the person with the strongest personality does. Men will often defer to women when it comes to decorating because it has traditionally been a woman's role. But traditional roles are changing rapidly and men should have their say in colour choices. It is their environment, too, and they should be comfortable with the choices.

Chances are that palette preferences will vary within a family, but there are several solutions. If each person has his or her own bedroom, obviously that room could be done in the occupant's preferred colourtime. When rooms are shared, such as bedrooms or mutual living areas, the people involved have to reach a compromise.

When two people live together and one is drawn to Sunrise colours and the other to Sunset, they may wind up fighting tooth and nail over every lampshade and toothbrush holder. I have been called in to mediate several such locked-horn situations. I find that the happiest solution for people from these opposite colourtime palettes is to compromise with lighter and deeper values of the Sunlight colourtime, since that palette overlaps into both of the others.

Because the Sunlight palette does not contain the vivid colourings of Sunrise or Sunset, it is the palette lest apt to offend. If you are a Sunrise compromising with a Sunset, and each of you feels the need for a splash of brilliance somewhere, use the guideline of dominance and subordination and you'll both be happy. Do the room (or house) in a dominant Sunlight colour and pull in a subordinate bright touch from either the Sunrise or Sunset palette.

Another effective, perhaps more pleasing compromise is to use crossover colours in combinations. Since crossovers are part of every colourtime, most people can relate to them and feel comfortable with them. For example: Wine, or aubergine, or raisin and grey might be used with a touch of sky blue. Or navy and taupe could be combined with accents of true red. Evergreen and sky blue might be brightened by a hint of sunlight yellow.

Monochromatic neutrals can also be effective compromises for people in differing colourtimes. Do remember to use a variety of textures and surfaces or these neutrals can become very monotonous.

Rooms That Flow

Rooms other than bedrooms can also be done in the colourtime of the person who spends the most time in that room. If you spend a lot of time in the kitchen and love to cook, you really should surround yourself with the colourtime that pleases you the most. If cooking is more of a chore than a pleasure, you might be even more eager to surround yourself with a pleasing colourtime palette.

If the man of the house loves to watch TV and relax in the family room he is entitled to be surrounded by the colours he likes best. I firmly believe that

Sunset (P.M.) *Fool-Proof Combinations*

The twenty-four combinations illustrated here are among the best 'fool-proof' possibilities in the Sunset palette. Some are classic and conservative – best for a business suit – like monochromatic Terra Cotta and Camel. Others are more fun – great for a jogging suit – like Paprika and Peacock. Choose whatever combinations suit the occasion, but try to use these suggested combinations to open yourself up to all the possibilities of your palette. For example, the best way to update khaki pants is to wear them with a brick red shirt. You'll have instant pizazz!

Bronze / Curry
Hunter / Peach
Bordeaux / Warm Taupe
Avocado / Khaki
Raisin / Ash Rose
Deep Teal Green / Cream White
Terra Cotta / Camel
Bay Leaf / Brick Red
Aubergine / Cadet Blue
Paprika / Apricot
Magenta Haze / Smoke Grey
Geranium / Sand

Plate O

If you want to stretch your budget, use neutrals and basic colours. Make taupes, beiges, greys, or deep basic shades like aubergine, raisin, wine, brown, navy, and charcoal part of your combinations. They are all classic colours that will work especially well as accessories.

For successful balance, one colour should be dominant, the second subordinate and the third an accent. Any colour in your palette's combinations may be the dominant, subordinate or accent colour. See Chapters 2, 3 and 4 for a complete discussion on combining more than three colours, plus additional 'how-to's' for your clothing and interiors.

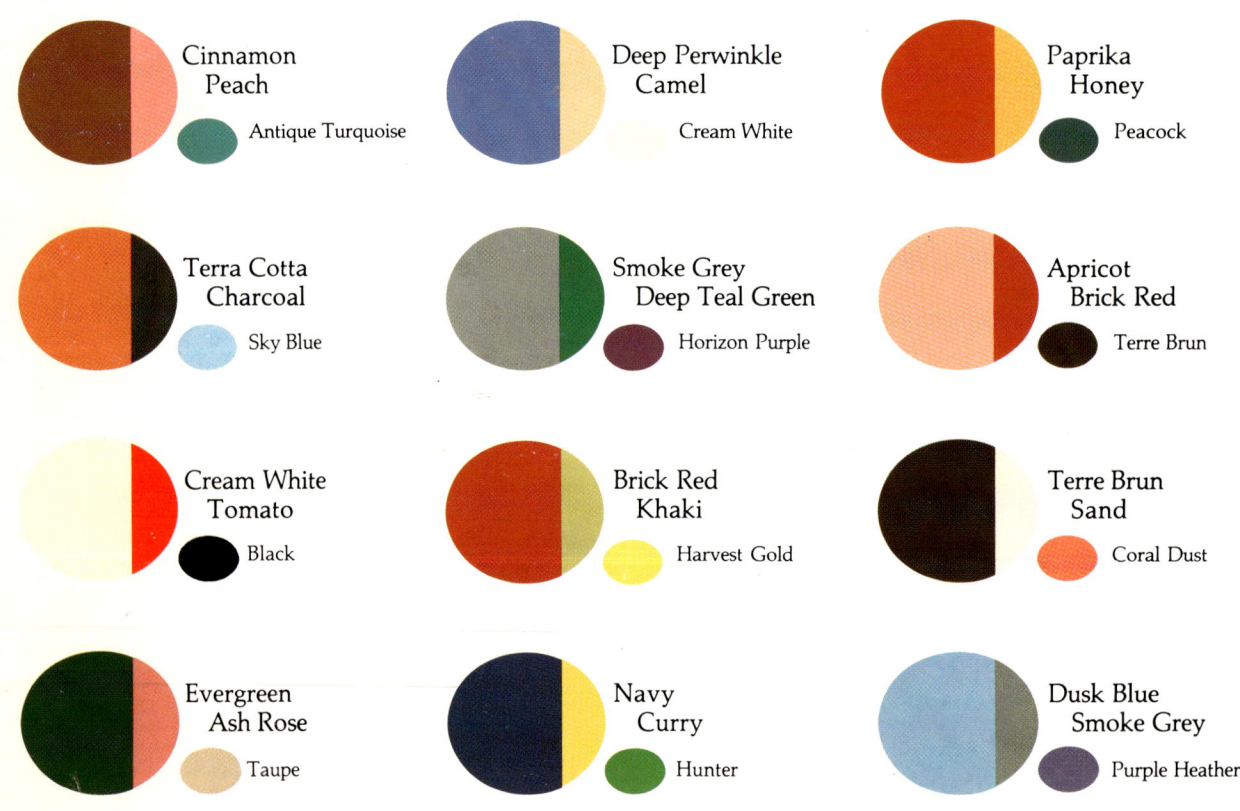

children should be allowed to participate in colour choices for their rooms, as long as they are not ridiculously bizarre. If your teenager requests punk rock purple and neon green, you might have trouble with your reaction, but their rooms are their private domains and, to use a cliche, we all need our own 'space,' as well as our own colours.

Bedrooms are rarely visible from the living room area, especially if the doors are kept closed, so you really don't have to be concerned about the colour scheme used in the rest of the house. You're not likely to use the same colours in a baby's room that you use in your own bedroom, so you can give everyone his or her favourite colours in the bedrooms. If a den is not visible from the living area, it may be done in a different colourtime than the rest. Think of the people who are going to use each room, and of the mood you are trying to convey in that space.

If however you have an open floor plan and many rooms are visible from a central point, or you live in a small home or apartment, you do want to keep a thread of colourtime continuity winding through your rooms. Your eye will find a natural pathway, and the rooms will flow one into the other, creating the illusion of more space. The same is true of adjacent rooms where one room is visible from the next, such as a kitchen that adjoins a family room, bedrooms and adjoining baths, entryways, and living rooms.

In open floor plans, or in small apartments or townhouses, the ideal solution is to connect your rooms without handling your colour combinations in exactly the same way. Reverse your colourtime schemes as you progress from one area to another. For example, if your living room was done in an AM combination of dominant emerald, with mauve morn as the secondary colour, the colour scheme could be reversed in the adjoining dining room area to make mauve morn dominant and emerald subordinate.

Increasing Colour Confidence

Beware of the spouse or flatmate who tells you to go ahead and decorate in whatever colour you like. The day the first piece of furniture arrives, you may hear something like 'Why in the world did you choose *that* colour?' I have heard many women say, 'My husband couldn't care less what colours I use.' Unless he is colour blind (which is in fact a possibility), he will have some sensivitiy to colour.

Have him look at the three pages of colourtime palettes and ask him to name his favourite. If he still says he couldn't care less, take him to an eye doctor and go ahead and make your own choices. He can't complain later that you didn't ask his opinion.

What about the neighbour or friend who comes into the house and says, after looking at the new chair you just bought, 'Do you really like that colour?' If the colour is 'new' and quite different from your usual safe choices, and your confidence is a little shaky to begin with, you can be demolished by a comment like that.

Don't let such remarks throw you. If you have used your preference quiz as a guide and shopped with your colour swatches so that you're not relying on memory alone, you can be confident enough to rely on your own judgement.

Just remember that people's opinions tend to be based on their own colour preferences. Have you ever stopped with a friend, considered something in a colour that you really weren't sure of and heard the friend say, 'Oh, I love that colour; you have to have it!' That is exactly what he or she means — they love that colour and it's probably in their favourite colourtime.

I wouldn't want to break up a beautiful friendship, but it is difficult for most people to be really objective about colour unless they are trained professionals with enough experience to be truly objective. Most people can't help but respond to colour on a subjective level. Chances are that if you take your friend's advice, when you get the colour home you'll never really feel comfortable with it.

You are better off following your own instinct and reinforcing that instinct with your colourtime swatches. That way you won't end up with an expensive mistake. If you do shop with another person, try someone with a really objective eye, or someone else in your colourtime!

After you've gotten feedback from family and/or roommates and decided on a colourtime in a particular setting, where do you go from there? The next step in decorating is to choose your main colour from within that colourtime. If you must decorate around existing colours, such as a carpet that has to stay, then you must obviously consider that carpet colour in terms of your scheme and move on from there.

In getting your colour picture together, start with:

1. the major or dominant area of walls and floor, then move on to colours for:

2. the secondary area of window treatments and larger upholstered pieces. Last come:

3. the accent pieces of pillows, occasional chairs, and other accessories.

Perhaps you have favourite objects — dishes in the china cabinet in a wedgewood blue — that will inspire a colour scheme. Or perhaps you have found a chair in a printed fabric that includes all your colourtime harmonies. All you have to do is expand on those harmonies to complete the room.

Sources of Inspiration

There are at least twenty directions to take in your search for ideas on developing a colour scheme.

Sunrise (AM)

Sparkling crystals
The sophistication of mirrors, glass, polished chromes; the starkness of black and white with one strong accent.

Clean, clear water colours
If you love the ocean blues and blue-greens, seafoam green, cool neutrals, and the white-caps of the waves, this is a good place to start. Although they are traditional for bedrooms because of their serenity, these AM colours will work in a living room.

Gemstones
Exciting brilliants in sparkling tones of sapphires, rubies, or emeralds.

The dawning of a new day
Cool greys, bright reds, and a flash of a vivid daybreak yellow.

Pure primaries, paintbox and jelly bean colours
Exciting brilliants, active, whimsical, and childlike. Unsophisticated and good for playrooms and children.

Sunlight (Midday)

A field of fresh spring flowers
The whitewashed brilliance of a meadow in full sunlight. Lilacs, wisteria, orange blossoms, and mint.

Delicious tints and shadings
Fruits and berries, ice cream, sherbet and confection colours. Plum cordials, peach melbas, and buttercream.

Desert sands
Soft and sun-bleached beiges and taupes with muted accents of sage, rosewood, or celadon.

Mother of pearl, seashells, and sand
Iridescent mauves, light peaches and greys, taupes and soft whites, soft turquoise, Limoges blue.

Sunset (PM)

Country and mountain
Warm burnished woods, hearth, home, herbs, heather, and homebaked bread. Hunter greens, warm browns, harvest gold, honey, cream whites.

Dusk
Mellowed, dusky blues, greyed purples, teal, periwinkle, and grey-greens of a sky at nightfall.

Sunset and Fire
The deep warmth of fiery shades of burnt orange, warm, intense geranium reds, horizon purples, and magenta haze.

Exotic and Spicy
Paprika, cinnamon, dill, and curry in paisleys mixed with bronze.

Southwestern American Indian
Terra cotta, clay, Navajo red, and antique turquoise set against silver.

All Colourtimes

These could be in any of the appropriate blending colourtimes. I'm sure you can think of more. All you have to do is keep your eyes, and your mind, open.

The great outdoors – If you are an outdoor person and love nature scenes, crossover evergreen and lush plants can provide a fresh, tranquil background. Floral patterns from any colourtime will blend with versatile evergreen.

Favourite objects – Ruby glass, shells, an antique coffee mill surrounded by the appropriate colourtime.

Travel mementos – Wall hangings, a throw rug.

A piece of sculpture, a painting, or a poster – Use the colours of a piece of artwork you already own, or take a trip to a museum for inspiration.

A room setting in the home furnishings department of a department store or decorator's shop.

A decorating book or magazine.

A beautiful wall covering, a bedspread, a scarf, or piece of clothing in a striking pattern that catches your eye can inspire a colour scheme.

Eliminating Expensive Mistakes

When you have decided on the colourtime you will use, and the dominant colour from that colourtime, you are then ready to use the colour wheel to decide which combination to use – monochromatic, duochromatic, etc. The best advice I can give you is to work with colour swatches for every single thing you do. This is the most efficient way to check the harmony of your colour scheme.

The size of the swatches should relate to the way the colours will be used in the actual room. Make your dominant colour the large swatch, the subordinate colour a little more than half that size, and your accent colours a scant one-fourth of the largest swatch.

Put them all against a white poster board. Use double-sided cellophane tape for easy removal in case you change your mind. It's so much easier to work this way than with bits of tattered wallpaper and unraveling fabric pinned to paint chips!

It's important to remember that bright colours appear even more so in large doses. The paint chip in the store will look very different when it's on all four walls. I always suggest to clients that they invest in a can of paint, do a section of one wall and let it dry thoroughly (preferably overnight) in order to really judge the colour. A cool blue in a small chip might turn icy cold on a wall.

It is really worth the time and effort it takes to gather good-sized samples of possible colours and patterns to see how they blend, particularly in the light of the room they're to be used in. A client I met recently told me that prior to my working with her, she had done her den in a red and navy colonial combination. She ordered her red and navy houndstooth couch from a small swatch. The day they delivered her expensive new acquisition, she almost suffered cardiac arrest. It was a lovely shade of purple. Red and blue do mix at a distance. Colours tend to merge even when you're just a few feet away.

Purple can be used as a touch with its red and blue neighbors on the colour wheel, but not in an area as large as the sofa. She wanted a duochromatic combination, and wound up with a trichomatic divided almost equally between red, navy, and purple. She eventually had it re-upholdstered because it was so obtrusive in the room. It was an expensive mistake that never would have happened if she had gotten a large swatch and viewed it from a distance next to the other colours.

Climbing The Wrong-Coloured Walls

The colours of the walls and ceiling (including windows and doors) are critical to the success of any room. They are the background that sets the stage for the room's atmosphere, and often account for more than two thirds of the available space. Your biggest wall-treatment decision will be: Do you want the walls to remain in the background, or do you want them to be a major element of the decor? Generally the more colourful the other furnishings are, the less colour you need in the walls.

Business manager **David Flynn** and his wife, actress **Jane Seymour,** live in a house in the Hollywood Hills that *Vogue* refers to as 'lightfilled.' It is, to be more exact, 'sunlight-palette filled.'

This beautiful airy house is done in a background of eggshell and light beiges in walls and furniture. Touches of luscious pastels are sprinkled against the neutral backdrop – misty greyed-green, lilac, and pale melon.

The dining room is done in light peach and blue with terra cotta tile; natural wood tones are used throughout. Baby Katherine's room is a Sunrise colour-time fantasy of what a little girl's room might look like. It's done with white wicker furniture and white eyelet on the trundle bed. Lollipop reds, yellows, blues, and pinks are used as accents and her lamp is a white duck with a cheerful yellow bill that lights up!

Your paint brush can become a magic wand. A fresh coat of paint can make an instant transformation and give a clean, new look. If you are stretching your budget, it is the least expensive way to redecorate. The more coats of paint you use, the truer the colour will be. Yellows and pastel pinks often need three coats; two coats will do for most other colours. Remember that colour intensifies and becomes darker than the paint chip when applied to the wall.

Use your colourtime swatches in order to make a pleasing choice for your walls. If the colour of this dominant influence doesn't blend with the other colours in the palette you've chosen, you'll feel like climbing the walls rather than living with them!

Uncommon Solutions for Common Problems

Painted surfaces can work magic through optical illusion. Walls may be moved without benefit of bulldozers. You may raise the roof or shrink a couch. Nooks and crannies may mysteriously disappear, or reappear to house an interesting object.

It is best to use a light background in a small room and to keep the window treatment light and airy so that the area is not too cut up. However, a small, dark space like a hallway, entry, or, alcove can be dramatized by doing just the opposite and making the colour intense or sparkly. Colours that would be overwhelming in rooms in which you spend a great deal of time can be energizing in small doses.

Deep or vivid shades are most effective in a passageway when it leads to a large, light area – the effect is that of a light at the end of a tunnel.

If you want to lengthen a short hallway or passage, paint the walls a deep tone and keep the floor and ceiling light. Place pictures along the wall in frames to match the ceiling or floor colour. This forms a horizontal pattern that the eye will follow to create more length.

In order to open up a cramped space, lighten the hue on the wall you want to expand. For example, if a lounge chair must be placed on a short wall, lighten both the wall behind it and the wall immediately opposite. The two remaining walls may be darkened to a medium or deeper tone. The same technique works for a narrow room. Paint the narrow walls lighter than the wider wall.

To make a square room less box-like, do one wall in a deeper tone than the other three walls. Dark or warm wall colours enclose a room, light or cool colours open it up. The same principle can be applied to any colourtime, since each palette contains both warm and cool colours.

Monochromatic and neutral schemes unify the space in a small room and give it the illusion of greater size. A ceiling will appear higher if it is painted white or a shade lighter than the walls – white or pale colours also give the best light reflection. Simply add white to your wall colour and use it on the ceiling. If you opt for white, use the white that blends best with your colourtime scheme.

If you want to lower the ceiling, paint it one tone deeper than the walls. Painting a wide band of the ceiling colour around the top part of the walls will also give the illusion of a lower ceiling.

To enlarge small windows, use the same shadings as the walls in your window treatment. Mini-blinds and shutters all have built-in vertical or horizontal lines and are excellent expanders. Don't use anything heavy on small windows and allow as much light to come in as possible.

In smaller rooms, it is best to keep the woodwork the same colour as the walls. Contrasting colours will break the wall into sections. In larger rooms, woodwork can be used as an interesting contrast, especially if it is embellished, and it can become a charming focal point. In a dull entry or hallway, brightly coloured doors can add some cheer.

If an area seems to cluttered with jutting protrusions, such as alcoves, dormers, bookcases, or window seats, do both walls and protrusions in a unifying colour. You can turn jigs and jags into interesting room features. A dark alcove, for instance, can be transformed into a dramatic background for some special object or personal treasure – especially if the background is done in a contrasting colour.

Who says pipes can't be beautiful? Ask any plumber. Pipes, plumbing, and duct work can be turned into eye catchers, instead of eyesores. Instead of fighting them, make them focal points.

Wallcoverings can also give instant colour and a marvellous ambiance to a room. Whatever the mood you want to convey – cozy, whimsical, formal, informal, glamorous – there are wallcoverings to express it. Flaws can be concealed and you often get more character with a wallcovering than with a painted surface.

Another big advantage, if you are a do-it-yourselfer, is that even a novice can teach herself to hang paper. However, if you are not good at matching patterns or cutting a straight line, leave it to the experts because a botched-up job can really look bad.

Striped papers with contrasting values can create height or width in a room. Colour placed effectively in a design can also create a rhythmic flow to draw the eye vertically or horizontally and increase the illusion of room size. Large design and deep, dark colours make a room appear smaller. Light solid colours and small designs make a room look larger. Many wallcoverings come with companion fabrics so that windows and walls can be coordinated for a more spacious look. The fabrics may be also be used in upholstered pieces to unify the room's design.

Foil and mylar papers can brighten as they add depth and interest. They can also visually increase size because of their mirror-like effect. Natural wallcoverings such as burlap, jute, grasscloth, and cork will work with any colourtime palette because they are neutral, but because of their warmth are more often used in Midday and PM palettes, especially in studies, offices, and entryways.

Avoid trendy colour combinations in wallpapers or any pattern for interiors, especially in equal proportions of the opposite colourtimes of AM and PM. Do you remember Sunset golden orange and Sunrise shocking blue-pink? That kind of look gets old very quickly. Whenever possible, start with the wallcovering, colour and pattern first, and then choose your ceiling and trim colours to blend.

It is also important to choose carpeting that coordinates well with the colours in the colourtime you have selected, because it occupies so much space and helps to set the mood of a room. Be sure to check a large carpet sample in daylight (the smallest it should be is fifteen centimetres square) as well as under the artificial lighting of the room setting, since the texture and colour are also affected by lighting. Multicolour carpeting can set the colourtime of a room and you can draw wonderful shadings from oriente land area rugs to integrate into your rooms.

Tips on Texture

Colour can be greatly affected and altered by texture because of light absorption and light reflection. A newly vacuumed soft pile carpet is a good example of this. Shiny surfaces intensify colour. Rough weaves deepen colour. The same colour appears brighter in polished cotton than it does in rough wool.

Matte or flat surfaces absorb light and appear somewhat darker than glossy, light-reflecting surfaces. Colours appear lighter and more lustrous on smooth surfaces that have a sheen. Apricot on a satin pillow will seem much brighter than the apricot cotton loveseat it sits on.

If, for an accent colour, you are going to dip into a different colourtime than the dominant palette you are using, choose a nappy or shiny changeable texture and the shade will blend better than it would in a dull texture. The changeability of the texture will also give variety to the colour and make it more versatile and less apt to offend the eye. For that reason, lustrous silks and synthetics, velvets, velours, velveteens, and polished cottons span the colour clock more easily than flat, non-reflective surfaces do.

Patterned For Success

Gone are the days of never combining patterns in the same room, but there are still a few guidelines to consider:

1. If patterns are not similar, such as a flamestitched needlepoint pillow on a floral chair, but contain the same colours, they will work together. Colour is the common thread that links them to each other.

2. Similar patterns will also work, but are more interesting if the scale is different. For example, a large check couch done in PM dusk blue could be used with a small houndstooth-checked chair done in the same colours.

3. Patterns appear 'heavier' than plain fabrics.

4. Remember that the colours of small-patterned fabrics and tweeds tend to blend. A pink and yellow sprig of flowers seen from up close can turn into peach just a few feet away.

Wood panelling, flooring, and furniture can add more pattern to a room but, just as with the other crossover colours in nature, the blues of the sky and the greens of plants, natural wood finishes do not intrude into an environment. Brown is the colour of bark and stems and twigs. The eye is accustomed to the many browns that surround us, so a variety of wood tones will harmonize and wood becomes a neutral. The polished surfaces and grains also show undertones that blend with all of the colourtimes.

Metallic finishes combine best with specific colourtimes. Sunrise colours work best with high gloss, cool tones of silver, chrome, and platinum. Burnished coppers, antiqued golds, bronze, pewter, and antiqued silver work best with the mellow Sunset colours. Brass and gold are metallic versions of crossover sunlight yellow and blend with all palettes. The Sunlight palette combines best with low lustre surfaces.

Shiny surfaces often pick up and reflect surrounding colours. For example, a glass and chrome table that usually works best with the AM palette will pick up and reflect the very warm tones of a PM brick red carpeting. Metals are more versatile than painted surfaces because of their reflective quality. Always think in terms of how the colours surrounding metal finishes will affect the colour of the metal.

Some antiqued or matte-finished metals reflect very little, if any, of their surroundings. Deep coppers will pick up very little of the coldest AM blues and purples. As a matter of fact, using the principle of complementary colour, cool blue colours will intensify copper because they are opposites on the colour wheel.

Alleviating Bedroom Boredom

The bedroom is often the last room in the house to be done because it's a fairly private place that others don't usually see. Our bedroom is the closest link to our backyard pool, so there are often hordes of teenagers traipsing through.

Sometimes the bedroom gets so loaded with magazines and books, and wardrobes so crammed with everything imaginable, that the thought of making more of a mess with paint or wallpaper simply overwhelms you.

Think of it as challenge. How well-organized and terrific you will feel when you empty the cupboards, throw all the mess away, and find things buried in bureau drawers that you haven't seen in years. You may even find your nightstand under that pile of books in the corner!

If you're not the messy type, but your bedroom has simply gotten boring and needs a little excitement, change the colours. If you want to stay within the same AM colourtime that you used before, simply switch from the traditional tranquilizing blues to more romantic sparkling wine and rose-pinks.

Colour in Interiors

A youthful, fun approach that combines all palettes – dominant *A.M.* Sapphire and Pure White on floors, walls and table; fabric coverings in Midday Peach Melba with a dollop of P.M. Burnt Orange. Photo courtesy Celanese Corporation.

The clean impact of a bedroom done in a analogous clear pinks, bittersweet, brown and white, particularly pleasing in the Sunrise *AM* palette.
Photo: Sears Roebuck and Company

The Grand Canyon colours of the *Sunlight* (Midday) palette – chestnut, sand accented with an analogous mixture of pillows in mauves, grapes, and soft blue.
Photo: Thomasville Furniture Industries Inc.

Plate Q

Colour in Interiors

Dining Room Setting

The warmth of the carpet, golden pine furnishings, Bordeaux sofas and walls, with a touch of Magenta Haze on the table shows a unique use of the Sunset *(P.M.)* palette.
Photo: Thomasville Furniture Industries Inc.

The opposite complementary shadings of Brick Reds, Browns and Peacock Blue set the cozy mood of this Sunset *(P.M.)* den.
Photo: Sears Roebuck and Company

A sophisticated bedroom of crossover Evergreen and Sand that works for *all* palettes. The pillow colours can be varied according to your tastes.
Photo: Thomasville Furniture Industries

Plate R

The Importance of Lighting

Just as in set design, the right lighting can set the stage to make a home more appealing and attractive. Since lighting affects your perception of colour, you should always check prospective colours in both natural and artificial light in the room where the colours will be used.

Daylight from an eastern exposure will intensify a colour slightly. When it comes from the south or west, it will redden a colour slightly. Northern daylight is the most neutral, and the best light for applying makeup.

There are two kinds of artificial lighting in general use. The most common is incandescent, the bulb that's readily available in any supermarket or hardware shop. Incandescent light does not radically change colours, but it does deaden them somewhat. A slightly ambered glow emanates from incandescent lighting, so that warm colours are enhanced and cool colours played down slightly.

Tinted incandescent bulbs are available. If you want to create a special mood, the general guideline is that each colour accents similar colours and subdues complementary colours. Aqua, green, and blue bulbs emphasize cool colours; yellow and pink intensifies warm colours. If you are using a predominantly cool AM palette or the cooler tones of Midday or PM, you may want to experiment with cool-tinted bulbs to see if you like the effect.

Tinted bulbs can add atmosphere to rooms done in neutral colour schemes. They can also add drama in a spotlight aimed at a focal point, such as a small art object or even a simple vase.

Fluorescent lights produce three to five times as much light as incandescents and are available in many varieties, ranging from cool to warm undertones. Soft white fluorescents blend best with incandescents for use in the home – particularly the deluxe warm white. Cool white is generally used in workshops, garages, and industrial plants. If you use fluorescents in the kitchen, the deluxe cool white gives the most accurate colour, but it's best used with the cool colours in each palette.

Themes and Schemes – Weddings and Parties

Colour is the most important part of what makes a party special. Using your colourtime combinations can make a table setting, a floral display, or a wedding party memorable and harmonious. The colours create the ambiance (and the beautiful photographs) that everyone remembers.

Just as in decorating interiors, the Colour Clock and the colour wheel are the two circles that get your creative wheels turning. The first choice is always made by deciding on a colourtime palette that will evoke the mood that you want to achieve.

You don't have to have a super-large budget if you use potted plants. You can go to your local nursery, choose whatever is in season and build your colourtime scheme around it. A pot of chrysanthemums in autumn can be surrounded by autumn leaves and sunset colours.

Favourite objects, such as a collection of old bottles made blue with water and a drop of food colouring, each with one flower or a bit of baby's breath, can inspire an AM setting. A plain philodendron can be given some unexpected glamour with three or four delicate real or silk flowers tucked randomly into the plant for a soft Sunlight look. A glass bowl full of colourful marbles makes an ideal base to push stems down into to keep them secure. It also gives you a colourful kaleidoscope of whatever colourtime pleases your fancy.

Weddings can be made even more beautiful by the use of the right colour combinations. Since the wedding party needs to be dressed harmoniously, this is not the time for individual colour choices, but the most important decision is: what colourtime is going to be the dominant theme?

The bride, traditionally, gets to choose the colours. Ideally, she will confer with everyone involved, but in the final analysis, she gets to choose. Somebody has to have the last word. Invariably, the bride chooses her own favourite colourtime. I've rarely seen it work any other way, unless there is a very domineering Mama or Mama-in-law involved.

Many grooms are now demanding equal say and playing a part in the whole process. Eventually (usually) everybody agrees and they all live happily ever after. However, it doesn't always happen that way. One couple asked me to arbitrate because they couldn't decide on wedding colours, furniture for the apartment, or the colour of the car they were going to share.

He was a Sunset and she was a Sunrise and both were very definite about their likes and dislikes. They compromised on the Sunlight palette, which seemed to satisfy them both. They invited me to the wedding. A few weeks later, I was un-invited. It seems that colours were not the only thing they couldn't agree on.

Most everyone in the wedding party can find a colour in the Sunlight palette that pleases them and its subtlety suits the occasion. Crossover colours are also a good compromise. Bridesmaids in wine or evergreen velvets and ushers in grey have become traditional in winter weddings.

Coordinate your flowers and table linens to go with the wedding party colours and everything will be beautiful. When you look back at the wedding pictures in years to come, it will be worth all of the effort.

I am reminded of one Hollywood wedding – the bride and the groom shall remain nameless — where the bride wore a lace dress that must have been worn in *Gone With The Wind*. It was miles of blushcoloured lace over an enormous hoop skirt. She also wore a huge picture hat.

There was barely enough room for her father to walk down the aisle with her, so he sort of trailed behind. It took the groom what seemed like a full five minutes manœuver around the skirt with the big hoop, so that he barely reached her lips for the final kiss, and almost knocked her hat off.

Her attendants all wore whatever colours they chose — a variety of vivid colours. It was definitely not what you would call subtle.

Other Occasions

For confirmation parties, Twenty-First's, engagement parties, and other special events, the colourtime used should be the one favoured by the honoree. The colourtime theme can start with the invitations and carry through the flowers and the rest of the decor.

If you are planning the party and the colourtime used is not your favourite, keep an open mind. Fashion coordinates and interior designers learn how to please their clients and often use colours they don't find personally pleasing.

After the colourtime is chosen, you decide on the dominant and subordinate colours within that colourtime. Then you refer to the colour wheel to decide on how you want to combine your colours. The procedure is much the same as it is in decorating a home. You must decide whether you are going to use:

One dominant colour *(monochromatic)*
Two colours *(one dominant and the other subordinate)*
Three colours *(one dominant, the second subordinate, the third, a touch)*
Multicolours *(polychromatic)*

Remember that the analogous colours are easy to combine. The complementaries will be the most attention getting when used in the brightest intensities (good for the bubble gum set).

Don't let the terminology scare you. Go back to Chapter Two and look at the Fool-Proof combinations. I suggest to clients that they use a colour board, much the same as the one described earlier. It really does help to use colour swatches to represent linens, flowers, candles, etc.

You can use paint chips that approximate your choices, if you don't want to cut the book up, just to see how the combination will look. It really is a fun, creative, exercise. It's just like being back in kindergarten with your paste and baby scissors (the kind you could never cut with). It's also marvellous therapy after a long, harrowing day. You may like it so much that you continue to do paste-ups after your party is over and all you're left with are wonderful memories, a photo album, and, of course, the bills.

Chapter 4

Men and Colour

Of course, everything I have said about colour in general applies to men as well as women. However, this is just a short chapter for men only, dealing with specific colour situations. I want, in this chapter, to make men more aware of the colour around them and its creative possibilities. It's not unmasculine to want to make the best of yourself and your surroundings. As we will see in later chapters, colour says alot about you and can influence your life in many ways, from the impression you make at that interview to how the colour of your office walls affects your working relationships!

We'll begin with the colour immediately around you.

Men and Hair Colour

Refer to the section on hair colour in Chapter Two. These same general guidelines also apply to men. Although there is still something of a stigma attached to the use of hair colouring by men, acceptance of this practice is growing rapidly.

If you are colouring your hair because of your self-image, if it makes you feel better about yourself, or if greying hair makes you feel older and you don't like the feeling, by all means do it! But please remember that grey or white hair can be very attractive. Look at Cary Grant, John Forsythe, and Bob Hawke.

If you do colour your hair, you must be willing to make the commitment to keep it up regularly. Regrowth of the unwanted colour looks obvious and unkempt. A slight 'highlighting' or streaking is often better than a solid shade – regrowth is far less obvious and you can go for a longer period of time without recolouring. It is also best for men to stay with subtle colours. Please – no severe blue-blacks after 30. It looks like shoe polish on the head, and the starkness draws attention to less-than-youthful skin.

As we age, our skin picks up lines and yellow pigment, and may become spotty. Hair colour should thus be 'softer' to de-emphasize these changes. Do not try to duplicate the exact shade that you had at age twenty. The haircolour that's gorgeous on a twenty-five year old can be a disaster at age fifty.

Suiting Yourself

When I do colour swatches for a male client, I give him many of the same shades that I give my female clients in the same colourtime. Many areas of a man's wardrobe give him the chance to experience the fun and creativity that colour can bring. Jogging suits, cushy velour tops and robes, sportswear, and emblem knit shirts can be bought in every colour of the rainbow.

In spite of having more freedom in dress and clothing colours than ever before, most men still need to dress conservatively for business. So I give them their basic colours, just as I give them to female clients, including the shirting that blends best with their colouring.

I find that the best colours for a man to build a business wardrobe around are the crossover colours. They work for all palettes and there is enough variety to keep a wardrobe from getting dull. You can always spark it up with a shirt in your own palette like a soft mauve, a light lavender, or a deep peach. But you can stay within the framework of the most basic crossover colours and have a very workable, acceptable wardrobe.

The staples, of course, are Grey Flannel, charcoal, navy, black, and variations of brown. Wine, aubergine, raisin, evergreen, and true red can be used as accent colours in ties and handkerchiefs. Sand, taupe, light grey, sky blue, and yellow make excellent shirting colours, both as solids and in combinations.

The crossovers are also the source of 'Power' colours, which you'll find out about in Chapter Five. Since the crossover colours work for all palettes, I usually suggest suit and/or jacket colours on the basics of hair. Grey and navy are excellent with grey, black, blonde, or silver hair, as are variations of brown with brown and red hair. Eyes and skin are often the source of shirt and/or tie colour.

Robert Redford wears his PM browns and beiges handsomely and favours leather and suedes. And **Paul Newman** is terrific in his AM blues and grey.

The most common mistakes made in coordinating a wardrobe are:

1. TOO MONOCHROMATIC – Light grey suit, pale blue shirt, pale blue tie.

2. TOO MANY DIRECTIONAL PATTERNS – Weaves, stripes, and patterns, each headed in a different direction.

3. WRONG MOOD – Sporty shirt with business suit.

4. WRONG TEXTURE – Silky tie with heavy wool suit.

5. WRONG COLOURS – Too many colours from opposite colour-times.

Among the combinations that will always work when in doubt are:

1. Solid suit, patterned shirt, solid tie

2. Solid suit, patterned tie, solid shirt

3. Solid suit, solid shirt, solid tie – if one element is colourful or contrasting, as with a dark blue suit, off-white shirt, and wine tie.

Other possible combinations for men include:

1. A solid suit with a patterned shirt and patterned tie if one is non-directional, or soft and quiet. For example: A solid gey suit with a light grey and white pinstripe shirt and a tie in a small paisley print of soft colours, including grey. The tie will always look coordinated when its pattern includes the colours of the suit and/or shirt.

2. A rep tie is acceptable with a striped shirt because it is traditional, your eye is accustomed to this combination, and because diagonal lines are neither vertical nor horizontal. But the colours and textures must blend.

If you do not have a good eye for combinations, or simply want to play it safe, don't put two patterns together. Pick up the colours of the suit or shirt in the tie.

If the suit is in a pattern, such as a weave or houndstooth, it is best worn with a solid shirt and solid tie. For example: A grey houndstooth suit with a light grey shirt and medium grey tie. If the pattern is very muted, a solid shirt with a subtly-patterned tie is possible. A pinstripe suit looks best with a solid shirt and tie, but you could use a tie with a subtle pattern. For example: A navy pinstripe suit with a white shirt and a navy and white tie in a small polka dot. If the pinstripe is hardly discernible, a narrow stripe shirt is possible, but with a solid tie. It is best to wear solids with tweeds to keep from looking too 'busy.'

Some fashion authorities feel that men's socks should match, blend, or relate to tie colour. For example: A red and silver grey striped tie with deep wine socks. Bright red socks would be a bit much – wine is a better choice. They are related to the red in the tie and won't scream at you. Another example would be a sky blue and taupe tie with navy socks. Sky blue is related to navy – and light blue in socks is inappropriate. Light socks give a casual look to an outfit, so they are not right for business or dress wear. I feel that you're always 'safe' with the darkest sock colours. If you're not wearing a tie, your socks should match your shoes.

Shirt patterns should be low key and subtle. Against a pale background such colours as brown, wine, grey, dark blue, and even black can work in a patterned shirt but bright colours, such as red, orange, purple, or bright pinks are cheap looking. They can be great for sportswear, but not for a conservative business look.

A touch of brightness sparks a dark tie. Pure white or a dab of colour can lift a dark suit, but the area should be small and restricted to the pattern, not the background.

Solids and small patterns are best — small polka dots, narrow stripes, small geometrics, miniature plaids, and subtle paisleys. In general, the fewer the colours, the more formal the tie. A coloured or patterned handkerchief in the breast pocket can be added for a touch of colour. It should relate to the tie colour. Vests can provide a good 'pulled together' look. Not only do they disguise a bay window, but when vest and pants match, the body appears taller and slimmer.

If you're a conventional dresser, or work in a conservative industry, black and brown are your best shoe shades. But if you like to experiment, or you're in a 'glamour' industry, try the neutral shoe colours, especially in warm climates or weather, or for sportswear. Remember, lighter neutrals work only with lighter coloured clothing. Check back with your colourtime palette on the colour pages in the front of the book, then choose your favourite shades, bearing in mind their suitability, from the Fool-Proof Combinations section.

Lastly, it might be difficult for you to relate to colours with 'feminine' names like Shocking Pink or Misted Rose. Just think of those vivid cotton knit sport shirts or button down oxford shirts in candy colours and you'll get the idea. Forget the names — just use your palette as your guide.

After all, women have been using so-called masculine colours like hunter green, cadet blue and navy for years, and it doesn't make us any less ladylike.

Living With Colour

In my experience, men, generally, take less of an interest in colour decorating than women. Even if a male client is eager to discover his own colourtime and co-ordinate his wardrobe accordingly, he will still tend to leave the broader decorating, in the home or office, to his wife, girlfriend or any other influential woman in his life. Of course, some men have an excellent eye for colour as do some women but, in general, men have a less developed education in colour and more prejudices than women.

Steve M. told me he would never wear lavender. In his culture, it was the colour of genteel older women. How could he, a macho man, relinquish his masculinity to lavender?

Years ago, there really were lots of little old ladies with sprigs of lavender at the throat and hair of a matching hue, but today grandma is more apt to be jogging around in pink sneakers and a lavender warm-up suit. Many men have gone beyond associating delicacy with pink and lavender and use both colours for button-down shirts and emblem T-shirts, with terrific results. But I'm afraid Steve won't be one of them. He's too hung up on lavender's association with old lace.

In my experience, women are more likely than men to have pleasant colour associations, and men are more apt to be indifferent to many colours. It could be that little girls have traditionally been encouraged to spend docile playtimes with colouring books, whereas boys are spurred on to active pursuits. Little girls are also apt to shop with Mummy, watch her make colour choices, and use her as a role model.

When it comes to decorating, men tend to defer to women. Because of this, many men must find themselves living in an unsuitable, even disturbing colourtime.

A man in a recent convention audience stood up in front of a collage that he was obviously uncomfortable with. His body language was the giveaway – he kept edging away from the collage and would never really look directly at it. When I asked him why he would choose a colourtime that he really didn't like, he said that those were the colours that his wife always decorated the house (and him) with. I asked him to bring her up from the audience, but he told me that would be a little difficult – she had been dead for ten years!

That poor, dear man was hanging on to the same old colours because his wife had been a very strong lady and he had allowed her to do his choosing for him. He just didn't know how to make his own choices and stayed with the old familiar ones out of habit. Are you doing the same?

Take an interest in colour. You probably have a substantial financial interest in your home, so it's important that you feel as happy and relaxed in it as possible. There is no reason why the wife should be the exclusive decorator, simply because she is a woman. Always, in marriage, partners should take on different tasks on the basis of ability, not sex. If your wife or girlfriend is going to take the major role in decorating, ensure that you are consulted and have alternatives and suggestions if you feel uncomfortable with the suggested colour scheme.

Many men prefer deeper, earthy tones, so if your spouse or lover is an AM pastel-lover, you are quite likely to shy away from her colours. As always, in these cases, I recommend that you compromise on the muted tones of the Sunlight palette and find colours together which best express your personality and preferences. Be warned. The price you pay for indifference may be ending up with an aqua bedroom when you would probably feel more comfortable (and more romantic) in a warm plumb bedroom.

Part II

What Colour Says About You

Chapter 5

Using Colour To Influence Others

Yang or Yin?

Colour is a very effective form of communication. We say a lot about ourselves through the colours we use. Circle the words below that you feel reflect your personality.

Extrovert	Introvert
Animated	Quiet
Intense	Relaxed
Realistic	Idealistic
Forceful	Gentle
Dramatic	Reserved
Direct	Subtle
Active	Passive
Analytical	Intuitive
Assertive	Submissive
Exuberant	Calm

    The words listed above are divided into two columns because they are opposites. The words on the left describe 'yang' traits; those on the right are 'yin' traits. The yang is thought to be more forceful and active, the yin more gentle or passive.

The terms come from the ancient Chinese who believed that each person is a blend of two personalities, the yang and the yin. These opposite characteristics, when put together, make up the whole balanced person.

How much of your personality is yang and how much is yin? Look at the descriptive words you have circled in each category. Add up your yangs and your yins. Did you circle more traits in one column than in the other?

Nearly everyone is a composite of both, because within the framework of your 'type,' your moods may change. The tiger in the outside world may be a kitten at home (or vice-versa!). Colours have personalities, too. Every colourtime has both yang and yin colours. You simply vary the shadings according to the mood you want to convey.

If you want to express a yin mood, use the light to medium colours. If you want to express a yang mood, use the brighter or darker colours. Every hue ranges in mood from yin through yang. The lightest reds are pink. They are yin – soft, easy, non-threatening. The brighter reds are attention-getting yangs. The deeper wine-reds carry more authority and weight. They are also yang, but with added dignity.

You may not be aware that you are expressing a mood when you choose the colours of the clothing you are putting together, but you really are. Have you ever tried shopping on a day when you weren't feeling too good about yourself? Melancholy moods make it difficult to come home with anything in a colour that you like. Try to do your shopping on a day when you are feeling 'up,' but if you can't always plan it that way, take your colourtime swatches to at least help you avoid mistakes.

Wearing light colours – or deep or bright colours – all of the time can get monotonous. Just as you try to keep a balance in your personality, you should work toward balance in your clothing choices too. The words that you circle might change from month to month or even from day to day, depending on what's going on in your life.

Nothing can get a change of personality over faster to the rest of the world than a change of colours. Bryan R., one of my clients, a bachelor in his mid-40's, had been dodging marriage to his ladyfriend, Laura K., for about five years. She came to me to have her colours done and told me that she had had enough of this longstanding relationship with no engagement ring in sight. Laura was ready to make some changes in her life, but she needed a little encouragement.

She started by bringing some crossover true reds and orange blossoms into her sunlight palette to liven up the light greys and beiges she often wore. She had lovely hazel eyes with lots of blue-green in them. I suggested teal, a colour she had never worn before, to enhance her eye colour. She had always used pale aquas – pretty for lingerie and soft summer dresses – but she needed more pizazz for her new colour personality.

I also suggested that she weave several blonde shades, ash and gold-beige, into her mousey-brown hair to get some colour variation next to her skin.

I'm sure you've guessed the end of the story. They were married in a matter of months… Laura in a teal dress, Bryan in a light grey suit (with a teal tie).

At one time, yang traits were considered exclusively masculine, and yin characteristics were women's territory. Today we are less apt to classify colour meanings by sex. Men are less reluctant to reveal their gentler side and women less afraid to exhibit assertiveness. Men wear pastel pink shirts and still come across as very masculine, and women can wear dark, tailored pants without losing their femininity.

Yang and yin colours can be combined. It is more difficult than staying with just one mood, but again, the secret is balance. An aubergine business suit in a very tailored mood can be softened by a mauve blouse with a ruffle at the neck. The suit is yang; the blouse is yin. It is true that most males styles are yang, but occasionally some yin breaks through. I have seen many macho macho types like **Burt Reynolds, Kenny Rogers** and **Clint Eastwood** on formal evenings with ruffled yin pastel dress shirts under their yang black tuxedos. Can you imagine those he-man types ever wearing a ruffled shirt with a pair of jeans? Yet it's perfectly acceptable for formal wear. They're probably the last of the holdovers from the days of powdered wigs and satin waistcoats.

The yang navy blazer can be worn with a light blue shirt for a touch of yin contrast. When you change colours to suit changing moods, be sure your choice suits the occasion. A kelly green T-shirt may be great on a golf course, but all wrong in a dignified courtroom.

Most performers know how to use colour to get their message across. When Olivia Newton-John first performed on stage, she wore floaty, feminine fashions in the delicate shades of her Sunlight colourtime. As her musical career was channelled into a more dynamic, assertive direction, she switched to brighter yang reds and blacks.

Highly shiny metallics are very attention-getting yangs and are often used for theatrical effects. Broadway and Hollywood producer **Hillard Elkins** told me the story of how a chorus girl became a star by changing the colour of her costume. During the production of *Golden Boy*, starring **Sammy Davis, Jr.,** a scene that should have worked didn't.

Hilly asked the set designer to go for some brighter colours in the costuming – to 'heat it up and add some gold for excitement.' The designer did just that and put a very talented chorus girl in unforgetably slinky gold lamé pants. The scene magically came to life, and **Lola Falana** rose to stardom in the show.

You may feel that some physical liability limits the colours you can wear. Don't let the fact that you're heavier than you'd like to be commit you to a life of the 'blahs.' You don't have to wear dark yang colours all the time to reflect your yang moods — add a touch of brightness from your palette, preferably close to the face, to give you a spark.

If you have light colouring, especially in the Sunrise palette, you may feel overwhelmed by the brighter colours in your colourtime. A touch of those colours in a tie, a scarf, or a piece of jewellery, or, for women, makeup shades can be a way to experience a wider range of your palette. The same is true for light skins in the Sunset colourtime.

Shy or reserved people often have trouble handling the brighter yang shades for obvious reasons. But colour can work to your advantage if you're shy — use a touch of a bright yang colour and people will be drawn to you. At a party, you won't have to break the ice first — someone else will, because colours work like a magnet to draw others to you.

Interiors have personalities, too. A contemporary room done in a predominantly yang mood would be a room of strong contrasts, such as a charcoal grey flannel-covered lounge against pearl grey walls and carpeting, with strong accents of true red. Chrome, glass, and lacquered surfaces would be in sharp contrast to the matte grey flannel. Colourful abstract paintings, large paisleys, or bold prints are also yang — they make dramatic statements, as do high-tech designs and plastics.

A room done in a yin mood would be much less dramatic. Its colours would be quieter. Contrasts would be subtle. Smaller prints, lace curtains, and traditional decor and artwork are yin. A country kitchen with gingham curtains at the window is yin. A young girl's room done in soft, sunny yellows with a canopied bed and fluffy eyelet pillows is yin.

Yang and yin can be combined in a room. It is more difficult to combine them than to stay with just one mood, but again, the secret is balance. Just as with personality, one type will dominate. Never split a room down the middle or you will wind up with a room with a split personality. Dominance and subordination are the key — approximately 75 percent should be one type, and 25 percent the other. A mixture of moods and styles is called 'eclectic' and many combine contemporary and antique pieces, but one mood should dominate.

Power Colours

A lot of attention has been given recently to colour in clothing for business. I do agree with the 'wardrobe engineers' who say that dark shades carry authority. The darker, basic yang colours carry more weight and convey an aura of power. The most powerful colours for men are navy, and dark or medium grey. Solid black for daytime is considered sombre in men's suits and is associated with undertakers. A touch of black in slacks, sweaters, or ties works for daytime, but black suits are for more formal wear.

There is still a hint of country associated with brown. It is dark and dependable, and solid as the earth, but some men in large cosmopolitan areas stay away from it because they do not feel it is 'citified' enough. They will go for it in leather or suede, but not in a suit or jacket.

Among the stars dressed for films by costume designer **Vicki Sanchez** are **Marsha Mason, Valerie Perrine, James Caan, Jack Nicholson, Jon Voight,** and **John Travolta.** She told me that in costuming for serious, powerful roles, she uses grey and navy. But she says that brown could be used for power on the man who is trying to disarm everyone who thinking that he is just a 'good ole boy' before he comes in for the kill (sounds like **J.R.** on *Dallas*!). She uses nondescript washed-out tints on insipid, powerless characters.

Power colours for PM palettes include paprika, bordeaux, terra cotta, deep tans, deep khaki, and avocado. Middays can use sages, bark, and chestnut, but the AM palette has to be careful of combining these earthy tones with AM colours. If you like those colours (and you usually don't), limit their use to touches. AM's may also use cocoa and bittersweet.

The lighter neutrals of sand, beige, light tans and greys, and light khakis and camels are not as powerful for either sex as the deeper values are, but they are appropriate substitutes in summer or in warm climates.

I have done many corporate seminars on suitable clothing for business men and women. The president of a large company called me in to try to upgrade the image of his sales force. His particular problem was that most of his salespeople were accustomed to the casual Los Angeles lifestyle and their clothing colours were just not credible for selling a prestige service, especially in conservative northeastern states.

A few of the men were resistant to change (the women were not), but most of the men were receptive to changing their wardrobes to the more powerful, deeper tones. Their sales increased along with their credibility.

When clients come to me to have their colours done, I always explain that basic colours are the most practical. Some colours come and go, depending on fashion's whim, but basics are here forever. They are the dependable, serviceable standbys.

But basics can get boring, so for business wear I suggest a touch of pizazz near the face. For men, a touch of colour in the tie, for women a blouse, jewellery, or scarf in a becoming colour that radiates into the face can add just the right impact. Which colours are your impact colours? The ones in your colour-time that are your true favourites – and the most becoming.

Try something different in combinations of power colours. Instead of the cliche-look of a brown suit with a beige blouse, try a brown suit with a rose blouse or navy with teal. The basic suit conveys the power and the impact colour is used next to the face.

Men, unfortunately, are much more limited than women in colour choices, but there are general ways to break the sameness habit. Navy blazers are great basics, but why not try a pink oxford button-down (from your colourtime) shirt, crossover grey slacks, and a tie that contains all three colours? The power of navy is predominant, but the pink adds a welcome creative touch.

Study the colours in your preferred colourtime. Stretch your imagination and look for new combinations. The simplest method for finding interesting colour combinations is to line all of your colours up and start playing with various possibilities. It will open you up to new and colourful ways of thinking, and it is really a very creative exercise.

Power colours have been used effectively for many years in uniforms. Dark blue is the most universal of all uniform colours – it connotes all of the dependable messages of blue, but with the added strength and solemnity of black. In many areas, tans and khakis are issued in summer to replace the traditional dark blue policeman's uniforms. Although lighter in colour, they still carry a military look and suggest aggressive action if necessary. Black shirts and uniforms are forbidding and scary. They remind us of SS men and Darth Vader and create fear rather than inspire confidence. Black is more acceptable as a uniform when trimmed with gold braid and worn with a white shirt.

The psychological message of a uniform of seems to inspire consumer confidence. Airlines have long recognized the importance of inspiring the confidence of passengers by keeping flight crews in darker power colours. In recent years, some airlines deviated by dressing female, flight attendants in cutesy miniskirts and garish colour combinations, but that stopped when the women's movement started. How can a passenger have confidence in a Barbie doll? The pendulum has swung back to efficient-looking uniforms.

The nursing profession has veered away from sterile whites into pastels. However, at UCLA's Medical Center emergency room, the nurses decided to experiment in an effort to shed the 'handmaiden' image and the subservient status that they feel is fostered by the medical profession's strict dress codes.

Instead of uniforms, they wear street clothes under white lab coats. Seventy percent of the patients polled felt that the nurses were warmer and more approachable, and that there was less of a barrier between them. It is interesting to note that they chose the white lab coat, which is still essentially a uniform, but one traditionally associated with doctors rather than nurses.

Surface Language

You never have another chance to make a first impression. Colour can help you make that initial meeting something special. We often want to make a special first impression, especially on social occasions, but the most important occasion is likely to be a job interview.

Dr. Leonard Zunin, a psychiatrist, has written a book called, *Contact: The First Four Minutes; An Intimate Guide to First Encounters.* In it, he talks about the four-minute time barrier, a time period in which initial human contact is established. If the initial reaction is negative, the eye and the mind start to wander to someone else.

When you are at a party and introduce yourself to a stranger, you begin a conversation. The first four minutes are spent in evaluating each other. We all do it, whether we admit it or not. TV commercials would have you believe that much of our negative reaction to others is based on the snowy dandruff on their shoulders, their yellow teeth, or the dark spots on their hands. As superficial as it seems, some of this is true. You do start to make judgments based on what you see – what Dr Zunin calls your 'surface language.'

He states that 'every colour and mode of dress can influence the direction of contact regardless of whether or not the assumptions we make are correct.' We dress not only to please our self-images, but to broadcast to others. Our tastes are vital clues to our personalities.

Personnel interviewers judge you by your verbal, body, and surface language. To improve on that initial contact, I always make the following suggestions about colour to anyone looking for a job.

1. Every business has a collective personality. Wear colours that are appropriate for that business. Obviously, a conservative power colour like navy or grey will work best for an interview with a top level industry, attorney, or accounting office.

2. If you're going for a job with a glamour industry, women can (and should) wear trendy shades to accent power colours. You will let them know that you know what is happening in the fashion field. Men can bring interesting colours into shirts and ties. Don't wear something unimaginative like a white shirt and a solid tie.

3. Men should avoid dark shirts and light ties with light suits for conservative companies. You'll look like something out of an old gangster movie.

4. Chances are you'll be one of many applicants. Try to make yourself a little more 'memorable' by using some interesting conversation piece of colour. For women, this is easy – a piece of jewellery, a smart scarf at the neck, or an impact colour in the blouse can help make you stand out from all the other applicants. For men, an interesting tie with a touch of colour and a pastel shirt will have to suffice, preferably in your signature colours, as described below.

5. Avoid colours that are generally turn-offs or 'tacky' brilliant. Overly vivid purples, brilliant oranges, garish yellow-greens, for example. You'll be memorable, but for the wrong reasons.

6. Wear colours that repeat or enhance your hair, skin, and eye colour. For example, if you have Midday streaked blonde-brown hair, hazel eyes that combine blue, green, and brown, and variegated rose and beige skin, wear a beige suit for your hair colour, a blue-green shirt for your eyes, and a tie or scarf of beige and blue-green with a touch of dusty rose. These are your 'signature' colours – a wonderful way to capitalize on your own colouring and make you stand out from the crowd. Everyone has a personal colour signature.

One of the best-dressed men in Hollywod often utilizes his signature colours. When I talked to **Robert Wagner** on the set of 'Hart To Hart,' I couldn't help but notice that his shirt matched his deep blue-grey eyes perfectly (his favourite colour is blue) and that his tan suit complemented his handsomely tanned skin. His tie combined both shades with a touch of off-white for contrast. His colourtime is Sunset.

What Your Place Says About You

Your home is an extension of you. It is your territory and reflects part of your personality. When I visit a client's home, I always look for clues that might help me to guide their colour choices. When people come to your home, they get a sense of you from the moment they walk through the door.

A colourless house has an austere, uninviting impact. Too many colours give a disorganized, jumbled impression. Too many cool colours with no warmth make a house unfriendly and aloof. Warm colours are instantly hospitable. If the colours get too warm or hot, however, the atmosphere can be overpoweringly stuffy.

Try to look at your setting with an objective eye. Do your colours really reflect you? Are you content and comfortable with your choices? Environmental psychologists tell us that people should live in environments designed to avoid anxiety-provoking colours. If you always feel slightly uneasy or uncomfortable in a particular room, the colours may be disturbing you.

Environments should enhance your psychological well-being. Expressing yourself in your surroundings is basic to your feeling of security – you feel 'rooted.' Self-expression through decorating a home is a form of therapy.

Working in an emotionally cold office can make you feel alienated, bored, and anxious. It's important to bring some personal belongings to work in order to feel comforted. Put a colourful photograph on your desk, or take a pet plant to work; anything to add a dash of colour and help you feel less depersonalized in sterile surroundings.

Communicating With Colour

The colours you choose for your personal and business stationery, business cards, flyers, and announcements all create an instant impression.

Most people will choose personal stationery in colours that blend with their favourite colourtime. **Lynn Redgrave** uses personal stationery embossed with a monogram several shades deeper than her beautiful burnished red hair. Lynn has that wonderfully unusual Sunset colouring of coppery hair, light cream skin with a peachy undertone, and peacock blue eyes. She tells me that she likes the earth tones and her favourite colours are autumn golds, dusky blues, and peaches, which are the undertones of her own personal colouring. She also favours dusky lilacs and creams, golden brown dogs, and honey-coloured kittens!

Joan Collins favours peach-coloured stationery. Peach invariably gives a message of instant warmth. Her stationery is a warm yin, but the characters she often plays are fiery yangs! At a fashion show she hosted recently, she wore a bright crossover true red suit with matching hat and I couldn't help but notice that her green eyes looked greener than ever against the complementary red.

For business stationery and cards, I suggest using the colours that best express the kind of business you're involved in. White is classic, of course, with black print for the letterhead. But it is rather ordinary, and certainly not as arresting as colours are. The tints used do not have to be blatant to be interesting.

If you want to convey the message that you are:

Cool, conservative, efficient	Light crossover neutral greys with contrasting darker grey, black, or deep wine print
Understated and cool, but more interesting	Light blue with navy print Light green with dark green print
Warmer, yet still understated	Creams and beiges with brown print Soft yellow with brown print

Fashion-oriented, but subtle	Interesting Midday combinations, such as lilac and mauve
Cosmetics-oriented	Flattering skin tones in all colourtimes, such as roses, pinks, peaches, and mochas with appropriate print
Stimulating and attention-getting (for flyers and special mailing pieces)	Bright colours of both Sunrise and Sunset palettes are especially good for announcements of sports activities such as exercise and dance classes.
Bold, daring and eyecatching	Combine the opposite palettes of Sunrise and Sunset for deliberate discord. Use complementary combinations like hot purple against yellow and no one will be able to ignore you!
Artistic and creative (florists, gift shops, designers, etc.)	Unusual colour combinations always reflect a flair. Discord is less desirable here, because to a prospective client, this is a preview of your work. Use pleasing but colourful combinations from all palettes; Midday is the best choice.

I recently spoke at a Direct Mail/Marketing Association convention, where I was shown some fascinating material on the benefits of using coloured and/or textured paper rather than pure white.

Test mailings included questionnaires, descriptive brochures, business reply cards and envelopes, order forms, and requests for contributions. Response rates for the coloured textured paper showed dramatic increases of from 7½ percent to 142 percent, underscoring the powerful force of colour in the marketplace.

Market testing indicates that your eye rests on a product for approximately .03 seconds as you speed along the supermarket aisle. So the message that you get and the association that you make with the product must be instantaneous.

Low-calorie sweeteners are in a pink pack to make them even sweeter. Fabric softeners are pastel to make them even softer. Bottled bleaches for even whiter whites are packaged in pure white plastic. You learn to expect that an aerosol in a green can will freshen the air better than an aerosol in a black can, and you are less apt to buy furniture polish in a purple can than in a brown one that suggests the richness of the wood.

Gold and silver in packaging give an aura of luxury and suggest quality. Wines, champagnes, and expensive chocolates are often foil wrapped. Yang black and gold used together are considered the ultimate in quality and sophistication.

Even simple little jelly beans are subject to market testing. Red and black have been found to be the most preferred, white and purple the least. Sweet makers are advised not to include more than 4 percent of these colours in their packages.

Colour has been known to increase productivity in industry. In a major manufacturing plant a colourful supergraphic was painted on a huge, formerly dull wall. Production increased by 8 percent. In addition, the restroom walls were painted a bilious green. That really got people back to their machines in a hurry!

Colour coding is a very effective way to keep office or home files organized for quick and easy recognition – especially at a distance. Stationery stores are full of colourful rainbows of red, green, blue, and yellow gummed dots and squares that can help you organize your life.

Prospective clients and customers start to make a judgement about what you have to offer them the moment they cross your threshold. The moment the door is opened your image is projected. You have to work even harder to overcome poor impressions if those first few moments of contact are not favourable (including the receptionist's welcoming smile and appropriate clothing!).

I often suggest to doctors, dentists, and therapists that their waiting rooms be done in calming colours. This is an ideal setting for the gentler Sunlight colourtime and provides a good balance of warmth and coolness. The extremes of the brilliant Sunrise blues or greens or the fiery Sunset reds and oranges would not be a good choice because they may stimulate rather than subdue a nervous patient.

Attorneys, accountants, bankers, and business managers can use monochromatic neutral beiges, taupes, and wood finishes and feel confident that they are always in good taste. The message is understated, careful, safe. Too much blue or green in this type of setting without some touch of warmth could come across as too cold and impersonal.

Power colours are excellent for serious business. The business management offices of **Traubner, Flynn, Philpott, Murphy, and Kress,** in Century City, California, are done in deep crossover evergreen (a good colour to associate with money), warm taupes, and a bit of navy, with touches of terra cotta and peach for needed warmth in a subtle print. This is a good, reassuring background message of responsibility and caring for their many top show business clients like **Warren Beatty, Goldie Hawn,** and **Paul Newman.**

We identify particular colours with certain names and products. Even if we cannot see the name on the package, we know that the neon yellow and red package contains **Kodak** film and we can spot a bright red and white striped box of chicken from the late colonel a half a street away.

If you need to make a choice about a business or personal colour signature, choose the palette first and then use the combinations in the colour section to help you make the decision.

Cars and Colours

Your automobile is an extension of your personality – an unspoken, but clear message to the rest of the world. The passenger in the sleek black limousine conveys a powerful and important 'yang' image. The macho driver aggressively darting in and out of traffic in a red Porsche probably fancies himself on the race course in Le Mans.

Distinctive car styles and colours provide wonderul opportunities for living out fantasies. The husband of one of my clients, a retired 65-year-old, drives a vintage Mustang painted a bold tomato red. He had always driven cars of nondescript grey or tan to his job with an insurance company. These sedate, low-key vehicles were part of his very conservative image.

He told me that when he retired, he realized that it was 'now or never.' The 'yang' in him could finally have its day. He chose tomato, the vivid red-orange in his Sunset colourtime, because it makes him really come alive when he gets behind the wheel.

Another client enjoys spotting unusual personalized number plate messages. On a recent cross-country trip he noticed one that he especially liked (the driver as well as the message). As he drove alongside a cute little AM blue Volkswagen Rabbit, he saw that the driver was a cute little AM blue-eyed blonde. As she drove ahead, he noticed that her number plate read 'Bunny.' Was that her name, he wondered, or did it simply go with the 'Rabbit'? Whatever the reason, her car was a strong reflection of her self-image.

If you're like most people, you choose your car colour with great care and deliberation and, if you have a good range of choices, will choose it in your favourite colourtime. We've come a long way from the days of Henry Ford who handled the question of car colour for his original Model T's by telling his customers that they could have any colour they wanted as long as it was black!

If you're the practical, thoughtful type who researches very carefully before buying, you might select your car's colour on the basis of its safety factor. The most visible colour is schoolbus-yellow. Orange shades also stand out, but at twilight or under foggy conditions, yellow, light beiges, cream, and white are more visible than orange. Yellow is strongly recommended for small compact cars because it visually increases their size. If you do drive a car in these highly visible colours, however, you'd better drive with care – you'll also be highly visible to the sharp-eyed highway patrol!

Some of the most popular shades of blue and brown are, unfortunately, among the least visible colours, and record high accident rates. Red cars would logically seem fairly safe because of the conspicuousness of the colour, but they too rate high in accident statistics. Red appears darker at twilight, and under most street lighting, seems almost dark brown.

White and off-white are suggested for warm climates, like Australia, because their reflective qualities keep interiors cooler; dark colours absorb heat. If you have your car repainted, it's wise to choose a colour that was standard for its make, model, and year. Choosing an off-colour could lower its trade-in or resale value.

Chapter 6

Your 'Shady' Past & 'Brilliant' Future

Your Colour Profile Quiz

The first part of this quiz deals with word association. Simply write the word or words that come immediately to mind. Do not change your original answer and do not linger over it. In the columns labelled 'Pleasant,' 'Unpleasant,' or 'Indifferent,' check your reaction to the colours listed. The words that you have chosen to describe the colours will help you to decide which column to check.

Colours	Word Association	Pleasant	Unpleasant	Indifferent
Royal Blue	Naval		✓	
Navy	blue	✓		
Sky Blue	harsh		✓	
Lavender	smell		✓	
Purple	pain		✓	
Yellow	pus		✓	
Orange	narch			✓

Colours	Word Association	Pleasant	Unpleasant	Indifferent
Peach	exciting	✓		
True Red	good	✓		
Soft Pink	luscious	✓		
Vivid Pink	punk			✓
Wine	soft	✓		
Brown	warm	✓		
Rust	soft	✓		
Bright Green	sour		✓	
Forest Green	enck		✓	
Olive	subtle	✓		
Blue-Green	swimming pool		✓	
Aqua	sea		✓	
White	heat	✓	✗	
Black	night	✓		
Grey	rain		✓	
Beige	sands	✓		
Taupe	warm	✓		
		12	11	1

Add up the marks under the 'Pleasant,' 'Unpleasant,' and 'Indifferent' categories.

Analyzing Your Answers

Were most of your marks in the 'pleasant' column? If so, you obviously, have a generally positive attitude toward colour. You are probably enthusiastic, well-adjusted, and enjoy many different colours. You are flexible and open to new experiences. You are likely to have been encouraged to play with crayons and paints as a child and loved it.

If more of your answers were in the 'unpleasant' category, you are somewhat closed to trying new colours and colour combinations. You are likely to be conservative, a bit opinionated, and have a difficult time expressing yourself with colour. Someone may have criticized you when your colours ran over the outlines of the drawings in your colouring book, and that same someone may have told you which colours to use where. But where there's life, there's hope. As you begin to understand why you have so many unpleasant associations, you will open up to the magical world of colour.

If most of your answers were in the 'indifferent' category, you've probably not had the opportunity to experience the creative use of colour. Perhaps you attended schools that emphasized the basics – where art was given low priority and most of your time was spent on the three 'R's.' You may be indecisive about choosing colours simply from lack of experience. You definitely need some pizazz in your life!

If your answers were equally divided between 'pleasant' and 'unpleasant,' with few or no 'indifferent,' you just need some encouragement. You are where the majority of people find themselves – in the middle.

Review your word associations on the quiz. For the most part, your words will describe feelings about a colour. For example, the usual reactions to blue include 'calm,' 'peaceful,' 'cool,' and 'water.' Blue sky tends to be pleasantly associated with clear days and the chance to enjoy being outdoors. It is the cool beauty of the reflection of sky on water, and the calm and constancy of the blue sky – although it may be dark and gloomy, we know that it's blue above the clouds.

Words associated with olive greens are usually grim rather than pleasant. Three frequent responses to this colour are 'army,' 'drab,' and 'sickness.' The word 'army' can be pleasant or unpleasant, depending on personal experience. But 'drab' connotes colourless, dull, negative feelings, which are intensified by the word 'sickness.'

At this point, you're not likely to know why you chose the words you did. Associations are not accidental – there is always an explanation. But your response is based on such 'ancient history' that you probably can't remember its cause.

One of my clients told me that he couldn't stand anything pineapple yellow. He couldn't stand to look at it, smell it, and least of all, eat it. I was really intrigued by this violent aversion and asked him to try to recall the event that caused his reaction.

Since he couldn't think of any reason for it, he asked his brother if he remembered anything that might have happened when they were children. His brother reminded him that as children they had each taken 25¢ from their mother's purse and splurged on pineapple sundaes. (Were sundaes ever really 25¢?) His brother also remembered that he had not only finished his own sundae, but went on to polish off the rest of his brother's.

Mother discovered the theft when they got home, but there was no need to punish them because they punished themselves by getting good and sick. The experience was only mildly traumatic, but it was enough to manifest itself in a long-term reaction to the colour involved. The incident illustrates how we can spend the better part of our adult lives depriving ourselves of a particular colour even though the reason has been lost to memory.

Many people have associated olive toned-greens with childhood illness. Biliousness and nausea are associated with yellowish greens, and we are said to 'turn green' when we are ill. Children are apt to associate illness with isolation, deprivation and yucky medicines – enough to turn them off to olive-greens for years, if not forever.

When you recall an incident that provoked a negative reaction, you can often begin to overcome your prejudice by recalling a balancing positive aspect. When my client who hated lavender recalled the pain of her grandmother's funeral, she also uncovered precious memories that had been swept out of her mind by the trauma of the event.

A little 'guided imagery' can help to overcome colour negativism. I suggested that my client with the pineaple in his past imagine himself on a beach in Hawaii with the ocean on one side and luxuriant pineapple fields on the other. He then suggested the addition of a lovely dark-haired Hawaiian lady with a try of Mai-Tais. Your fantasies can take you, too, to wondrous places!

Enticing the rainbow

Compare your answers to those on the following list. These are the words most used to describe the colours in the quiz. Most colours have negative, as well as positive, connotations. As you will see, there are many more positive than negative associations.

For every negative response you had on the quiz, try to think of a balancing positive. The purpose of this quiz is to help you to rewind that tape recorder in your head so that you can re-examine your thoughts about colour and open yourself up to that enticing rainbow.

Colours	Positive	Negative
Royal Blue	Flags, bright, kings, tropical ocean	Sharp
Navy	Uniforms, nautical, sea, conservative, service, sober	
Sky Blue	Heavenly, celestial, wet, cool, ice, peaceful	

Colours	Positive	Negative
Lavender	Delicate, nostalgia	Aging, insipid
Purple	Violets, royalty, mystical, artistic	Shadowy, mourning, melancholy
Yellow	Warm, friendly, radiant, sunshine, cheerful	Jaundice, cowardice
Orange	Glowing, bright, pumpkins, hot, harvest, juice, sunset	Too loud
Peach	Delicious, warm, inviting, ripe, fuzzy, juicy	
True Red	Hot, fire, intense, passion, energy, excitement, active	Rage, blood
Soft Pink	Feminine, icing, sweet, tender	Too sweet, cloying
Vivid Pink	Attention-getting, fun	Tacky, cheap
Wine	Rich, elegant, refined, tasty, velvet	
Brown	Earthy, dependable, secure, masculine	Dirty, soiled
Rust	Autumn, sunset	Rusty
Bright Green	Clear, moist, grass, St. Patrick's Day	Envy
Forest Green	Nature, cool, refreshing, restful	
Olive	Oil, army, tree	Drab, illness
Blue-Green	Ocean, clean, clear	
Aqua	Water, cool, refreshing, clean	Weak
White	Light, cool, clean, pure	Sterile
Black	Dark, night, sophisticated, sexy, dignified, serious	Mysterious, ominous, depressing, death
Grey	Flannel, neutral, rain, conservative, practical	Ghostly, somber, mousy
Beige	Warm, neutral, classic	Colourless
Taupe	Classic, neutral, practical	Colourless

The colours with the fewest negative connotations are usually sky blue, blue-green, forest green, navy, wine, and peach. This may be because of the positive thoughts they bring to mind: sky, ocean, forest, an alluring drink, a delicious fruit.

If your responses are very unlike those indicated, you are not strange – just different. And it is these differences that give us our individuality.

Most people discover that most of their favourable associations are in their preferred colourtime palette. Chances are your least favourable associations will also be in your least favoured colourtime.

The purpose of these colour exercises is to get you to analyze your responses, get rid of old prejudices, and open your mind to new colour possibilities. If, however, you continue to detest a colour (even though it's in your colourtime), do not use it. It may simply be too difficult to deal with and there are many other shades and tints for you to use. If you suffer from colour deprivation, it's not terminal – just tiresome!

The Colour Clones

When a colour story is new and popular, the market is often inundated with it, either alone or in combination with another 'now' colour. About 20 years ago, powder blue and olive green were worn together for the first time. I can remember going to my first 'Hollywood' party and feeling terribly unique and daring in that combination, only to find that the other five women present were wearing the identical colours!

High fashion colours can be exciting and novel, but become passé very quickly. Colour trends can lead to colour trouble. There is always a place for newness, but it should be used with caution. Bathrooms and bedrooms are good places for trendy colours since it is less expensive to change towels, bathroom carpets, and bedspreads than it is to redo an entire living/dining/family room area. Accessories, in interiors, clothing, personal stationery, table settings, linens, floral arrangements, and even in lighting, also provide relatively inexpensive opportunities to experiment with unique colour combinations.

Colour combinations often reflect historical periods and social trends, such as the 'psychedelics' of the 60's. The emergence of the 'hippie' counter-culture, political rebellion, dissonant rock music, the Beatles, pop art, and changing lifestyles found reflection in the bright oranges, luminous pinks, and neon greens used together during the period. But that kind of look can become tacky and dated very quickly.

Remember, you can only tolerate such screaming combinations for a short time.

It is fun to experiment with 'new' colours, especially those to which you reacted very favourably on the association quiz. They are emotionally stimulating and novelty is intriguing. However, familiar colours give you a feeling of comfort and security. You may want to stay with colours that are old friends. But don't just stay with them out of habit – do it because it feels right. Colour choices are often made because of peer and social pressure. If you make choices because of what is 'socially acceptable' in your community, you can become a colour clone whose house is either a boring replica of every other house on the street, or whose apartment looks like very other one in the building.

Do you allow other people to make your colour choices for you? Is it because you lack the confidence to make your own choices? It is often easier to defer to another person's judgement (and also avoid responsibility for the wrong choices).

We often seek colour opinions from other people, especially those whose taste we admire. There is nothing wrong with that, provided the other person is qualified to give advice. When you get unsolicited opinions, always consider the source. Remember, there are virtually no 'rights,' or 'wrongs.' It is simply a matter of how you choose to express yourself.

The guidelines and 'how to's' of combinations in this book are designed to give you greater confidence. If you stifle your creativity and basic feelings about colour, you will eventually regret it. If you chose a living room lounge because your daughter/husband/wife/mother-in-law/flatmate/friend told you that it was the colour you should have rather than because you liked it, you may regret not following your own instincts. You're also likely to end up resenting the advice-giver.

Likes, Dislikes, and Secret Desires

There are individual colours within each colourtime palette that you will like above all others. Every colour is included in every colourtime, in varying intensities and values. Each colour evokes a different emotional response from you.

If you really dislike a colour, it probably won't be in your preferred colourtime, but you could be the exception to the rule.

Refer to the page on which you wrote your favourite and least favourite colours. For your amazement and amusement, I have compiled what some of the experts, researchers and psychologists say about your colour choices and added some of my own experiences with clients.

Please remember that your likes and dislikes can and do change over the years. Your responses will simply tell you where you are in your life right now. Your preferences may also indicate some of your secret desires. For example, red is considered the most ardent and passionate of all colours. You may not see yourself as ardent or passionate, but if red is your favourite colour, maybe there are hidden traits just dying to be expressed (you little devil!).

Red

Like:
Just as red sits on top of the rainbow, you like to stay on top of things. You have a zest for life. Remember that red can speed up the pulse, increase the respiration rate, and raise blood pressure. It is associated with fire, heat, and blood, so it is impossible to ignore. And so are you (or would like to be).

The key words associated with red are winner, achiever, intense, impulsive, active, competitive, daring, aggressive. Red people are exciting, animated, optimistic, emotional, and extroverted. Desire is the key word (see 'ardent' and 'passionate' above), so they hunger for fullness of experience and living.

Now that you have all the good news, let's hear it for the bad news. Since you crave so much excitement in your life, routine can drive you bananas. Restlessness can make you fickle in your pursuit of new things to turn you on. It is hard for you to be objective and you can be opinionated. You have a tendency to listen to what others tell you and then do whatever you please. Patience is not one of your virtues.

However, you are an exciting person to be with, and always stimulating. The world would be a dull place without red people.

Dislike:
Since red is primarily associated with a zest for life, excitement, and passion, a dislike of this hue could mean that these feelings are a bit much for you to handle at this point in your life. Perhaps you are bothered by the aggressiveness and intensity that red signifies. Or perhaps you would really like more fulfillment but are afraid to get involved. People who are irritable, ill, exhausted, or bothered by many problems often reject red and turn to the calmer colours for rest and relaxation. They are very self-protective.

Pink

Like
This is a softened red, so it tempers passion with purity. It is associated with romance, sweetness, delicacy, refinement, and tenderness. Pink people are interested in the world around them, but they do not throw themselves into participating with the ardor of the red person. Violence in any form is upsetting to you.

At one time, pink was considered feminine, like the frosting on a little girl's birthday cake, but now it can be worn by men without embarrassment – after all, it is closely related to red.

If you love pink, you are talented and have subdued drive, charm, and warmth, and are probably an incurable romantic. Pink people, are friendly but tend to keep inner feelings hidden.

The closer to orange pink gets, the warmer it is, and you are.

Dislike
Soft, medium tints do not evoke much emotion – many people (especially men) are indifferent to pink. It is sweetness, innocence, and naiveté – red with the passion removed. So if you dislike pink, you are looking for excitement in your life and pink simply will not do it for you.

Yellow

Like
Yellow is luminous and warm because it is strongly associated with sunshine. It sparkles with optimistic activity. Yellow people are highly original, imaginative, idealistic, creative, artistic, and often spiritual. You love novelty and challenge and have an inquiring mind. You are a reliable friend and confidant. Your ambitions are often realized, and you usually have a sunny disposition.

You are often egostistical, however, and do not like to be second best. You can be generous, but may be rather shy at heart and appear somewhat aloof as a result. You may be impatient with other people's ideas if they seem less well thought out than yours. You are genuinely concerned about the good of society, but generally spend more time talking about it than actually doing anything about it! Yellow people are perfectionists, but can also be joyful.

Dislike
If you dislike yellow, you usually dislike the qualities that this luminous colour has. You are a realist – a practical, down-to-earth person and probably critical of others who are not. You are skeptical of new ideas and rather than try something innovative, you prefer to concentrate on things you know you can accomplish. Guaranteed results are important to you, because you like to protect yourself from disappointment.

Orange

Like
Orange is a combination of red and yellow, so it takes on many of the characteristics of both colours. It is vibrant and warm, like the autumn leaves. Orange has the physical force of red, but it is less intense, less passionate. Lovers of this colour work and play hard, are adventurous and enthusiastic.

You are good-natured, expansive, and extroverted with a disposition as bright as your favourite colour, and you like to be with people. Your ideas are unique and you have strong determination. You are more agreeable than aggressive, however, orange people can be fickle. It has been said that your latest friend is your best friend.

Success in business can come easily to this gregarious, charming person. Since orange is a physical and mental stimulant, start the day by eating an orange while dressed in your orange terry bathrobe, to start your mind and body working together!

Dislike
Life is definitely not a dish of gumdrops for the rejecter of orange. Nothing flamboyant appeals to you. You dislike too much partying, hilarity, loud laughter, showing off, and obvious intimacy. As a result, you may be difficult to get to know, if not a loner. You prefer a few genuine close friends to a large circle of acquaintants and once you make a friend, they're your friend forever.

Brown

Like
The colour of Mother Earth is the hue that is associated with substance and stability. A preference for brown means you have a steady, reliable character with a keen sense of duty and responsibility. You are the down-to-earth person with a subtle sense of humour. Browns love simplicity, comfort, quality, harmony, hearth, and home.

You are a loyal friend – understanding, but firm. Brown people have strong views and may be intolerant of others who think, talk, or act too quickly. You strive to be good money managers (we won't say 'cheap') and drive a good bargain.

You are the person who might find it difficult to be carefree and spontaneous but will often rebel internally against accepting things the way they are. You feel very uncomfortable about losing control, but will work hard to change a situation that seems unjust or unfair.

You'd make a good marriage partner and a good parent because you have a strong need for security and a sense of belonging. Family life is very important to you.

Dislike
You probably fantasize about a lot of things, perhaps travelling with a circus

or racing cars. Novelty excites you and routine drives you crazy. You are witty, impetuous, and generous. Living on a farm is not for you. Homespun people bore you. You do like people, but they must be bright and outgoing. A meaningful relationship with you could be risky business – it's hard to get you to sit still!

Beige

Like
Beige people have many of the same characteristics as brown, though they are probably less intense. Creamy beiges and honeyed tones take on a lot of yellow qualities, while rose beiges take on pink characteristics. You are warm, appreciate quality, and are carefully neutral in most situations. You are usually well-adjusted and practical.

Dislike
You are less frenetic and impetuous than a dislike of brown, but have many of the same characteristics. Beige represents to you a beige existence – boring and tiresome. You hate routine.

Green

Like
Nature's most plentiful colour promises a balance between warmth and coolness, so green people are usually stable and balanced types. This is the good citizen, concerned parent, involved neighbor, and P&C member – the joiner of clubs and organizations. You are fastidious, kind, and generous.

It is important for you to win the admiration of peers so you are often a 'do-gooder.' You are a caring companion, loyal friend, partner or lover, with a high moral sense, and are super sensitive to doing the right thing.

You are intelligent and understand new concepts. You are less inclined, however the risk something new than to do what is popular and conventional. The bad news about green people is that they often have big appetites for food. If you are dieting, it is difficult for you to lose your lumpies. The worst vice for a green is the tendency to gossip. Are you a little green with envy?

Dislike
Since lovers of green are usually very social, joiners, and 'keep up with the Jonese's' types, dislikers of green will often put those qualities down. You may have an unfulfilled need to be recognized that causes you to pull away from people rather than join them. You don't like thinking, looking, and doing

things the way you see the majority of people thinking, looking, and doing them. Picnics, cocktail parties, and Saturday night at the League's Club are not your thing.

Biliousness and certain body functions are often associated with yellow-green, as are snakes, lizards, dragons, and various other creepy-crawlies. Did something slithery frighten you as a child?

Blue

Like

The colour of tranquility and peace, blue tends to be the most preferred colour universally. Although cool and confident (or wishing to be), blues can be vulnerable. You are trusting and need to be trusted. You are sensitive to the needs of others and form strong attachments, and are deeply hurt if your trust has been betrayed.

Blue people aspire to harmony, serenity, patience, perseverance, and peace. You are somewhat social but prefer sticking to your own close circle of friends. You think twice before speaking or acting out. You are generally conservative, even-tempered, and reliable.

Because of the highly developed sense of responsibility of the blue personality, you must be careful of perfectionist tendencies that may make you unrealistically demanding. Your gentleness, however, will win out.

If you have trouble falling asleep at night, think of the blues in your colour-time, or count blue sheep.

Dislike

A dislike of blue may mean restlessness – a need to break away from the sameness that bores you. Perhaps you would like to change your job, or even your life, and long for more excitement. You might be tired of being 'dependent on,' but your conscience makes you stay. You wish that you were either wealthy or brilliant (or both) because that would enable you to have all the good things in life without working so hard. Deeper blues may mean sadness and melancholy to you – blue may simply give you the blues.

Blue-green

Like

Since this is a marriage of the colours previously mentioned, many of the traits will be combined, but there are added dimensions. You are neat (to the point of fussiness) and well-groomed. You are sensitive, but also sophisticated, self-assured, and (usually) stable.

You help others and usually manage your own affairs very well. Courtesy and charm are characteristics, too. But narcissism is a key word here. Green-blues love to dress up to get the admiration of others, but along with admiration, you may also provoke some of the 'blue-green-eyed monsters.'

Dislike
Since love of blue-green means orderliness and neatness, dislike of blue-green means that, as messy as you'd like to be, a little voice inside you (was it your mother or your father?) keeps telling you to clean up your room. As much as you try to ignore it, it won't go away. You would really love to relax more and not pay attention to petty details. You really prefer earthy types to fussy people.

Purple

Like
This hue has an aura of mystery and intrigue. The purple person is enigmatic and highly creative, with a quick perception of spiritual ideas. Purple is often preferred by artists. People who like to consider themselves different from the common herd or unconventional often prefer purple.

You are often generous and, at times, charming. Purple is also associated with wit, keen observation, super sensitivity, vanity, and moodiness. Because purple is a combination of red and blue, which are opposites in many ways, you often have conflicting traits. You are constantly trying to balance those opposites – the excitement of red with the tranquility of blue. It has been said that purple people are easy to live with but hard to know. You can be secretive, so that even when you seem to confide freely, your closest friends never completely understand you.

Dislike
If you are anti-purple, you need sincerity, honesty, and a lack of pretence in your life. You do not like to get involved unless you know exactly what you are getting yourself into. You usually exercise good judgement. Frankness is a quality you look for in your friends. You may not have a particular artistic talent, but you would make a good critic!

Because of purple's association with royalty, purple may seem puffed up and pompous to you, or because of its association with mourning, you may see it as melancholy. In certain areas of the world, bright purple is worn by ladies of questionable reputation. Perhaps you are still hearing that little voice in your ear telling you that nice people don't wear purple.

Lavender

Like
People who love this tint use it sometimes to the exclusion of all other colours. Just as with purple, this person likes to be considered different. You are quickwitted, though usually not intellectual.

The lavender person seeks refinement in life. Yours is a fantasy land where ugliness and the baser aspects of life are ignored. Outward appearances are very important. Gentility and sentimental leanings also go along with this colour, as do romance, nostalgia, and delicacy. Since lavender is first cousin to purple, you may aspire to creativity, but if not capable of it, you tend to encourage those who do have talent.

Dislike
Yours is a no-nonsense approach to life. You don't like others to be coy with you — you would rather they be direct. Nostalgia is not your thing; you live in the present. Just as with the anti-purple people, you don't like superficiality in manners or appearance and you usually let people know about it (or wish that you had).

Grey

Like
People who prefer this most neutral of all shades are carefully neutral about life. You like to protect yourself from the hectic world, wrapping yourself with the security blanket of a noncommittal colour. You prefer a secure, safe, balanced existence, and so, unlike the reds in life, you never crave real excitement, just contentment. It is important for you to maintain the status quo.

You have often made compromises in your lifestyle. You are practical and calm and do not like to attract attention. You are willing to work hard (the grey flannel suit) and to be of service. You are the middle-of-the-road type, cool, conservative, composed, and reliable.

If this makes you feel like a little grey mouse, the consolation is that you will often use a splash of colour to make some sort of statement. So you really aren't all that dull!

Dislike
To dislike grey is to dislike neutrality. You would rather be right or wrong, but never indifferent. Routine bores you. You look for a richer, fuller life. This may lead you to get into one involvement, hobby, or interest after another in

the pursuit of happiness. Grey may mean eerie ghosts, ashes, cobwebs, and the dust of a haunted house, or other scary grey things.

Taupe

Like
This colour also speaks of neutrality, but combines the character and dependability of grey with warmth of beige. You like classic looks and are careful about allowing too much excitement into your life. You're practical, fair, well-balanced, and would make a good arbitrator.

Dislike
If taupe doesn't appeal to you, it may be because it is so balanced and classic. You'd rather make a more definite statement, whether with colour or otherwise. You're probably not known for your subtleties.

White

Like
White is cleanliness and purity, and those who prefer white are neat and immaculate in their clothing and homes. You are inclined to be a cautious buyer and shrewd trader, but critical and fussy. If you got a spot on your tie or scarf in a restaurant, you would summon a glass of water immediately to clean it off. White also signifies a self-sufficient person and, occasionally, innocence. It is a recall of youth and simplicity.

Dislike
Since white represents cleanliness and purity, to dislike white does not exactly mean that you are a messy person, but it does mean that you have never been obsessed with order. You are not very fussy. Things that are a little off-centre are much more interesting to you than those that are perfectly in line. A little dust on the shelves or on yourself doesn't throw you into a spasm of cleaning. You are not very uptight and are easy to be with. You may see white as sterile and connect it with nurses' uniform, doctors, and worst of all (for many people), dentists.

Black

Like
This is rarely chosen as a favourite colour because it is actually the negation of colour. The person who chooses black may have a number of conflicting

attitudes. You may be conventional, conservative, and serious, or you may like to think of yourself as rather worldly or sophisticated, a cut above everyone else, or very dignified.

You may also want to have an air of mystery, or, as in the language of the proverbial black negligee, be very sexy. Wit, cleverness, personal security, and prestige are very important to you.

Dislike

Since black is the negation of colour, it may be a total negative to you. It is the eternal mystery, the bottomless pit, the black hole, the witch and her black cat. It may represent death and mourning to you. Things that go bump in the night are black. Were your frightened by the dark in your childhood? That experience could be buried in the darkest recesses of your mind and may still haunt you when you look at anything black. Black may simply be too heavy or depressing for you to handle at this point in your life.

You are uncomfortable with the super-sophisticated and feel insecure in their company. You like real people and are not dazzled by dignitaries.

Conclusion

Unless you live in a cave or a nudist camp, you have to wear clothes. Every day of your life you send messages out via your colours. Why not choose your very best colours for those messages, whether you're wearing a business suit or jogging suit? You're painting a picture for your own enjoyment that can't help but spill over to those around you.

Use your colourtime palettes as an expression of you, to help you feel more rested, energized, creative, and confident, and to make your home a true source of comfort. You deserve it.

I hope this book has given you useful and enjoyable information. Your life may never be the same – you may find yourself studying the celebrities on TV or the person in front of you at the check-out stand, and driving your friends, family, and salespeople crazy with your new-found knowledge. (Careful – lighting and makeup can be deceptive, so what you are seeing on the TV screen may be *reel* colouring instead of *real* colouring!) You're apt to look at the colours they choose – for their clothes, their kitchens, and their cars – with new insights. It can be great fun and a wonderful way to heighten your awareness of the world around you.

Use your colourtime palettes as an expression of the real you – from the colourtime that makes you look and feel your absolute best, to the colourtime ambiance you create in your surroundings. Make every day a special day... come alive – with colour!

Bibliography

Birren, Faber. *Colour, a Survey in Words and Pictures.* New Hyde Park, New York: University Books, 1963.
– *Colour in Your World.* New York: Macmillan Publishing Co., Inc., 1962.
– *Colour Psychology and Colour Therapy.* Secaucus, N.J.: Citadel Press, 1980.
Bornstein, Marc and Marks, Lawrence. 'Colour Revisionism.' *Psychology Today,* January 1982.
Graham, F. Lanier. *The Rainbow Book.* New York: Vintage Books, 1979.
Gross, Amy. 'How to Read a Person Like a Colouring Book.' *Mademoiselle Magazine,* March 1976.
The International Journal for Biosocial Research. 'The Effects of Colour Psycho-Dynamics, Environmental Modification Upon Psycho-Physiological and Behavioral Reactions of Severely Handicapped Children.' Vol. 3, 1982.
Luscher, Max. *Luscher Colour Test.* New York: Random House, 1969.
Molloy, John and Humber, Thomas. *Dress for Success.* New York: Warner Books, 1975.
Sharpe, Deborah T. *The Psychology of Colour and Design.* Chicago: Nelson-Hall Co., 1974.
Von Furstenburg, Egon with Duhe, Camille. *The Power Look.* New York: Holt, Rinehart, and Winston, 1978.
Worthy, Morgan. *Eye Colour, Sex, and Race – Keys to Human and Animal Behavior* Anderson, South Carolina: Droke House/Hallux, 1974.
Zunin, Leonard with Zunin, Natalie: *Contact, The First Four Minutes.* New York: Ballantine Books, 1973.

Index

Accessories, personal, 48-53
Ambiance, 29-31
An eye for colour, 25
Analagous colours, 39
Angell, Jeff, 55-56

Bacall, Lauren, 49
Bergen, Candice, 22
Brown, Bryan, 21

Carter, Linda, 15
Charles, Prince &, 22, Princess Diana, 20
Closet
    Organizing, 149-152
Collins, Joan, 100
Colour & Cars, 103
Colour Balance, 28-29
    Dominant & Subordinant, 34, 95
Colour Clock, 15
Colour Profile Quiz, 105, 108
Colourtime Quiz, 7, 11
    Explanation, 12-15
Colour Wheel, Plate B
Combining Palettes, 33-35
    Hybrids, 33
    Discord 33, 47-48
Complementary
    colours, 51
    & personal colouring, 39-41
    in interiors, 41
Cool colours, Plate Q, R
Cosmetics
    About, 51-53
    Changing palettes, 55-56
    Crossover makeup, 55
    Sunrise, 53
    Sunset, 54
    Sunlight, 54-55
Crossover Colours, 23-25
    Plate I, J

Decorating with colour, 71-85
    Bedrooms, 82
    Carpet, 80-81

Developing confidence, 73-74
Eliminating mistakes, 77
Metallic surfaces, 82
Problems & solutions, 78-80
Resolving differences, 72
Sunrise, 75
Sunset, 76
Sunlight, 75
Diller, Phyllis, 47-48
Duochromatic (two-colour) combinations, 42-43

Environments
    Intimate, 31-32
    Extended, 32
Evans, Linda, 15, 20

Falana, Lola, 94
Fenster, Fleur, 21
Flynn, David, 18
Fonda, Jane, 21
Fool-proof combinations, Plates I, J
    Sunrise, 61-64
    Sunlight, 67-68
    Sunset, 64-66

Gallaher, Simon, 20
Gibson, Mel, 20
Grant, Cary, 20

Hair tinting, 56-57
    Blondes, 57
    Redheads, 58
    Brown, 59
    Grey, 59-60
    Men, 86-87
Hawke, Bob, 22
Hepburn, Katharine, 22

Job interviews, 98-99

Lighting, 83
Little, Jeannie, 20

MacLaine, Shirley, 36
Marketing Colour, 101-102

Men's clothing
    Business colours, 87
    Common mistakes, 87-88
    What goes with what, 88-89
Midler, Bette, 48
Monet, Claude, 11
Mononchromatic colour, 41-42

Neutral colours, 45-46
Newman, Paul, 20, 87
Newsome, Debbie, 20
Newton-John, Olivia, 22, 94

Offices & waiting areas, 102-103

Personality & colour
    Yang & Yin, 92-95
    Yang & Yin in interiors, 95
Polychromatic (multi colours), 45
Power colours
    for men, 95-96
    for women, 97
    in films, 96
    uniforms, 97
Principal, Victoria, 21
Psychology of colour
    emotional impact, 27
    meanings of
        beige, 115
        black, 119-120
        blue, 116
        blue-green, 116-117
        brown, 114
        green, 115
        grey, 118
        lavender, 118
        orange 113-114
        pink, 112-113
        purple, 117
        taupe, 119
        white, 119
    what your place says about you, 99-100

Redford, Robert, 21

Remick, Lee, 22
Sarazin, Kay, 36
Savalas, Telly, 21
Scott, Walter, 30-31
Self-Image, 25
Seymour, Jane, 78
Skin
    Oriental,15
    Ruddy, 15
Somers, Daryl, 22
Stoner, Lynda, 21
Stationery
    Business, 100-101
    Personal, 100
Streisand, Barbra, 21, 30-31
Sunlight (Midday) Palette, 18, 21, 22
Sunrise (AM) Palette, 18, 19, 20
Sunset (PM) Palette, 18, 20, 21
Surface Language, 98
    First impressions, 98

Taberer, Maggie, 21
Taupe, 39, 42, 43
Taylor, Elizabeth, 20, 39
Trichromatics, 43-44
    Three-Colour combinations, 43

Undertones, 32-33

Wagner, Robert, 99
Warm Colours,
    Plates Q, R
Weddings & Parties, 41-42, 83-85
White
    Does not go with everything, 35-37
Women's clothing
    Belts, 50
    Handbags, 50
    Jewellery, 51
    Shoes, 48-49
    Stockings, 49-50

Yang & Yin, 92-95
    in interiors, 96

21.1.89

Pearl grey skirt - red shirt   ok.
                - pearl grey/pink shirt   good ✓
stripped pink shirt - navy short sleeved shirt   good ✓
navy short sleeved - long sleeve snob shirt   good
light blue t-shirt - stripped long-sleve blue shirt   good
cream cardigan - purple t-shirt
navy t-shirt - coffee shirt   good
apricot - light blue t-shirt   ok
                - cream cardigan (L. Ashley)   good ✓
                - white t-shirt   good ✓
                - navy t-shirt   good
                - blue sweater with yacht   good ✓
                - black sweater   good
                - apricot sweater (cotton)   good ✓

Images in Colour

If you would like a Fan Deck (50 colours) in your colourtime palette in an attractive pursue size carry-case for $25.00 send the coupon below

☐ Yes, please send my Fan Deck plus information on *colour courses* and accessories.
Cost: $25.00

I am a ☐ Sunrise

☐ Sunlight

☐ Sunset

☐ My cheque for A$25 is enclosed.
Made out to "Images in Colour".

Name: _____

Address: _____

_____ Postcode _____

Mail to: *Images in Colour*
P.O. Box 60,
St. Peters. 2044, NSW
AUSTRALIA